Breaking Ground

The History of Operating Engineers Local Union No. 3

by Charles S. Costello III, Mandy Jo Jessup,
Jamie Johnston, Jan Wissmar

M.T. Publishing Company, Inc.

P.O. Box 6802

Evansville, Indiana 47719-6802

www.mtpublishing.com

Graphic Designer: Elizabeth A. Dennis

Library of Congress
Control Number 2009934808

ISBN: 978-1-934729-25-0

Printed in the United States
of America

Out of 600 books printed this book is number __77__.

Photo on front cover: Operating a Bucyrus Erie Steam Shovel, engineers working on the Ocean Shore Railroad in California pose for this 1907 photo.
Photo on back cover: Operators step off their equipment for this group shot at the Rancho Murieta Training Center. (Courtesy of Charles Odell)

Top ▲ Hazardous road work in 1929. (Courtesy of Robert Lubke) Bottom ▲ High Track D10 at the New Melones Dam project. (Courtesy of Bob Beall) Opposite Page ▶ Rockface railroad at quarry in Richmond, California in 1920. (Courtesy of Igor Blake)

CONTENTS

DEDICATION

*Dedicated to the past, present and future generations
of Local 3 members who have committed their lives to stand up
and fight for the rights and values of the middle class.*

CURRENT OFFICERS

Russell E. Burns,
Business Manager

Fred D. Herschbach,
President

Carl L. Goff,
Vice President

James K. Sullivan,
Recording Corresponding Secretary

Dan D. Reding,
Financial Secretary

William K. Mahoe,
Treasurer

▼ *Miner George Gage (left) comes
off shift and talks with Chief Steward
Harold Hughes (center) and Business
Agent Bob Mayfield (right).*

ACKNOWLEDGEMENTS

Many people have contributed to this book project along the way, and it would be impossible to acknowledge everyone. So I would like to give a big thank you to the members who have contributed to this book project with their photos, their interviews, and their comments. A number of current and former Local 3 staff members contributed to this book providing research, photos, writing, and editing. Retiree Norris Casey began the initial research for this book project. Many retirees wanted to preserve the rich history for those who didn't live through it as they did. Linda Lawrence picked it up from there and was a huge help in organizing the information and doing some of the initial research.

This book had been planned for a number of years, and it finally came together in my office, an office that continued to collect dust, old photos, boxes of old pins, building dedication headstones, and more over the past few years. Business Manager Russ Burns deserves a lot of thanks for continuing on with a project that could have very well become a victim of the nation's economic downturn.

Finally, the following individuals contributed photos, memorabilia, or were subjected to interviews, some of which lasted hours. Thank you all for your years of service, loyalty, and solidarity to the labor movement and to Local 3:

Vernon Baumbach, John H. Beale III, Dominique Beilke, Jerry Bennett, Igor Blake, Curtis Brown, James Brown, Bill Burns, Russ Burns, Rod Cameron, Clarence Cleaver, Al Dalton, Jim Earp, Ken Edgecombe, John "Jack" Fitzgerald, Abraham Fontanilla, Alvin Foster, Gloria Gardener, William H. Genn, Jr., Carl Goff, Ken Green, Bernard Hammond, David Hardman, David Harlan, David Hayner, Frank Herrera, Tom Hester, Harold Huston, Douglas Jojo, Glenn Jones, Roy Kingery, Bob Leslie, Harold Lewis, Loring "Bud" Lintt, Robert Lubke, Leo Markey, Dale Marr, Bob Miller, Heidi Mills, Dennis Moreland, Gerald Muck, Lou Nisich Jr., Charles Odell, Linda Olivier, Harold Puckeylow, Paul Rasmussen, Marvin Reed, John Rhodes, Max Spurgeon, Tom "T. J." Stapleton, Gerald "Jerry" Steele, Sandy Steele, Russ Swanson, John Sweeney, Joe Wendt, Ted Wherry, Rob Wise, Charles Wright III.

— Charles S. Costello III

5

FOREWORD

by Russell E. Burns

I am thrilled and honored to be able to say some words on what has been an extraordinary seven-decades of history for Operating Engineers Local Union No. 3. It humbles me to have the opportunity to not only lead this great organization but to introduce this thoroughly researched and visually stunning look at our history appropriately titled *Breaking Ground*. The book summarizes our history, decade by decade, covering major projects and milestones, changes in our industry, state and national politics, and the internal struggles that are the makings of the seven decades of this great local union.

Russell E. Burns, business manager

We could never cover everything from our history in a book of this type but made every attempt to look at the early events that necessitated rivals coming together to form what is now Local 3. This book covers the significant dates, events, and struggles of the labor movement and gives us as an organization a chance to express our deep appreciation to those who built this great local.

It is important to pause and take a look at where we came from, and where we are going. History allows us to look in the mirror, to take our pulse and, in doing so, shed light on our present and investigate our vision of where we can go in the future as an organization. It allows us to laugh, to remember the good times and the bad, to tell stories, and to take a look at the many challenges that have been a part of the history of this incredible union.

Returning to our roots is extremely important to me because my family roots stretch over four generations of operators. My grandfather was a member, as was my father and now my son. I remember fondly the rides with my dad, starting when I was about 8 years old. You could never do it today, but I used to ride around on top of the tractors out there with my dad. Those days were different, they were special, and you can imagine what a thrill it was as a young boy to be able to do that. I remember those times riding with my dad very well. He instilled in me that sense of camaraderie that is so prevalent in the field and the work ethics that are such a crucial part of our culture and history.

This book reflects the extraordinary commitment of a union culture in which diversity and opportunities abound for those willing to get the training, put in the hours, and develop the skills to navigate the good and bad times that are part of the industry. It reflects the determination and willingness of a group of people to go the extra mile, to stand together on the picket lines, to sacrifice for the good of the whole, and to step up and demand change when change is needed.

The sights and sounds invoked by the voices, images, and stories of *Breaking Ground* bring the past to life. These voices are the voices of the founders, the brothers and sisters who paved the way for what has become the largest and strongest local in the history of the International Union of Operating Engineers (IUOE). The new sound we hear as we approach our 71st year is the sound of equipment running, the sound of our voices working together, the sound of hope, the sound of a nation going back to work to build, defend, and fight for the rights of the working class.

I hope you enjoy the book.

Russell E Burns

INTRODUCTION *by Charles S. Costello III*

Operating Engineers Local Union No. 3 was a union born of necessity. It was a necessity then and is a necessity now as anti-labor forces continue their assault on the working class. One might ask, why a history of the union? Because in times of great economic turmoil and hardship, it is more important than ever to clarify the roots and core values of any organization and the roots of labor go deep. I was a newcomer to union culture when I was hired by Local 3 in 2003, unlike so many members who are third- and fourth-generation members. But as this book evolved I was evermore impressed by the importance of history and the central role unions play in American democracy. Visiting job sites, attending district meetings, talking to retirees, listening to their stories, and walking the picket lines continually strengthened my appreciation of what it means to work for a union and to uphold the rights and privileges of labor that have helped build this great country.

Breaking Ground is the history of Local 3, a union that helped build the West as part of a labor movement that began in 1896 with the formation of the National Union of Steam Engineers of America, which continues today as the International Union of Operating Engineers (IUOE). It's the story of how a local union, founded during difficult and uncertain times, grew as the country braced for World War II, how a group of rivals came together after trying time and time again to join forces, and finally, how they weathered the good times and the bad to stand together in solidarity for the rights and values of the working class.

In the 1930s, the IUOE began to grant more and more union charters, making it harder to get work outside your local jurisdiction without paying doby (traveler dues) or being forced to "sit on the bench" waiting for work because you weren't a member of that local. As a result, workers were reluctant to teach anyone, except their most trusted co-worker, how to operate their equipment. This led to so many problems that, finally, in January 1939, the seeds were sewn for the March 1939 founding of Operating Engineers Local 3, otherwise known as "Local 3." From the original 1,000 members brought together with a common purpose, the local now represents more than 40,000 workers across four states that include northern California, northern Nevada, Utah, and the Hawaiian Islands.

For many working-class families, union membership spans generations, dating back to the early 1900s when great-grandfathers worked backbreaking hours for little pay in miserable working conditions. These men broke the ground

for today's members, fighting for labor's right to organize for better wages and working conditions. As in many great movements, Local 3 began with the realization that ordinary working people have the power to make great change if they stand together against a common foe—big business and the anti-labor forces that prey on the working class.

It all began in the midst of the Great Depression, when despite grim economic times, the West was still growing. Out of great difficulties often comes the necessity for change, although sometimes the change is not by choice. The election of Franklin D. Roosevelt in November 1932 brought hope of a return to happier days and the chance to strengthen the rights of the working class. During this time, two bridges were being built in the San Francisco Bay Area: the Golden Gate Bridge, using union labor, and the Bay Bridge, using mainly non-union labor. Work on these bridges signaled the economy was slowly turning around, but there were other problems, holdovers from the Depression.

Change was coming, but as news of a possible merger between the different locals floated in the wind, not everyone was ready or eager to join forces. On February 6, 1939, after the 21st International Convention held in Miami, Florida, news of the amalgamation was announced to the membership of Local 59, the largest local in the group. Considerable discussion followed a report from the delegates who attended the convention with one member making a motion to hold a smoker or caucus of sorts. His motion was called out of order by the president, his appeal lost, and a subsequent vote by the membership approved the delegates' action in Miami. Local 3 was born.

"Labor is prior to and independent of capital. Capital is only the fruits of labor, and could never have existed if labor had not first existed. Labor is the superior of capital and deserves much higher consideration. All that harms labor is treason to America. If any one man says he loves America but hates labor, he is a liar. . . there is no America without labor. . ."

Abraham Lincoln

10

Throughout its history, Local 3 would face many unforeseen challenges, including a world war, racial discrimination, internal corruption, the struggle for on-the-job safety legislation, and so much more. Changes brought about by a consent decree were an important step in bringing opportunities to an increasingly diversified membership. Equal opportunities meant that more and more women and minorities could take advantage of training opportunities, helping to form the most diversified workforce in the industry.

Breaking Ground examines Local 3's history, decade by decade, including a detailed look at the events that led up to the amalgamation in March 1939. Each decade had its own unique challenges. The 1940s paved the way for Local 3, as shortly after its amalgamation, it would become a powerful force in support of the war effort, leading up to and during World War II. After the Japanese surrender and the subsequent return of the soldiers to Local 3's jurisdiction, the long-awaited postwar boom finally materialized. This meant further growth for the now, more influential union. Dams, highways, and other infrastructure projects either stalled or in limbo during the war finally began. As its first decade came to an end, Local 3's jurisdiction would stretch across three western states and Hawaii—a territory at that time.

During the 1950s, Local 3's size and influence had grown to such a point that it was termed by the IUOE as the "West Coast International." But that growth and influence brought internal political struggles both at home and within the International Union, ultimately causing the downfall of Local 3's first business manager, Victor Swanson. The IUOE would also have its share of scandals. As a result of the Select Committee on Improper Activities in the Labor or Management Field (informally known as the McClellan Committee), the decade came to an end with all unions under a cloud of suspicion.

The 1960s began with Local 3 under IUOE supervision, but it quickly regained independence under Business Manager Al Clem. This decade was characterized by a focus on safety, training, and a number of large projects that helped union membership grow. The opening of the Rancho Murieta Training Center (RMTC) in 1969 and the subsequent building of that local community gave Local 3 hope in continued growth; however, the union was unprepared for the coming environmental movement, not to mention continued struggles with union politics.

Opposite Page ◀ Construction of the Colorado Street Bridge in Pasadena, California in 1912. (Courtesy of Douglas Jojo)

INTRODUCTION

The 1970s began with more growth but with a new set of challenges, including a growing environmentalist movement that put a stop to a number of projects or at least slowed their progress. Ultimately, Local 3 would have to make compromises as the environmental movement gradually altered the way big construction jobs were approved. Other challenges were internal ones, with the August 1972 election of Local 3 officers being contested and eventually ruled unlawful after a long and dragged-out series of investigations. Local 3 was forced to rerun the election, and in November 1973, Dale Marr was elected business manager.

The 1980s began with a changing of the guard on two fronts: the election of former California Governor Ronald Reagan as president of the United States, and the 1982 election of Tom Stapleton as business manager of Local 3. The new Reagan administration condoned unprecedented attacks on working men and women that would weaken the union. On the other hand, the election of Stapleton brought hope for beneficial changes to the union. Beginning with Marr and continuing under Stapleton, Local 3 agreed to address conditions that had plagued society for centuries with the establishment of a program to help members with alcohol and substance abuse problems.

The 1990s called for refocusing after 12 years of Republican attacks on labor. The alarming deterioration of labor's influence and the decline of union membership across the country had taken their toll on the working class, as the rich got richer and the poor got poorer. To make matters worse, general operating expenses continued to rise and Local 3 was running out of money. Business Manager Don Doser, who had taken the reigns from Stapleton in November 1996, would have to raise membership dues; however, this dues increase would not take place before union leadership took care of those who paved the way with a new pension program called "The Rule of 85." Soon after, a bylaws change approved by the membership allowed for supplemental dues and the ability to hire additional staff to service the membership.

The year 2000 arrived with a bang in the form of the Y2K bug and fears of doom for the computer systems across the world and at Local 3. This was just the beginning of a number of storms both figuratively and literally, as Local 3 and the world battled natural disasters, terrorist attacks, internal corruption, federal and state budget crises, and more. The seventh decade ended on a positive note though, with the election of Barack Obama and a hopeful return to the roots of labor, with the Employee Free Choice Act (EFCA) on the horizon.

Breaking Ground was written by a group of writers who worked diligently to pull this research together. After reading through handwritten meeting minutes that led up to the historic amalgamation, it was obvious why these many locals merged into one large organization. In addition to these meticulously handwritten early documents, research was gleaned from more than 66 years of the *Engineers News* and over 30 oral interviews of current and past members. To complete this historic publication, photos were gathered from the archives and combined with member-contributed photos.

Breaking Ground sheds light on the past while strengthening the sense of common purpose in the present. Throughout its history the labor movement has learned from its mistakes, and Local 3 is no exception. Along the way, Local 3 would inevitably ruffle the feathers of big government and big business, as the local resisted efforts to bust unions through legislation such as the Taft-Hartley law and state Right-to-Work initiatives. All union misdeeds would be scrutinized and foibles unveiled, but in the end, the ground had been broken, and Local 3 would survive.

The 70th year of Local 3's history is just one more storm to weather in the ongoing trials and tribulations of labor's struggle to represent the common ideals and values of a working class. Despite a world-wide economic meltdown brought on in large part by corporate greed, the election of Obama as the 44th president of the United States brings with it hope for a return to the ability to organize, to provide health care and benefits to a working population here at home instead of outsourced abroad. That means a return to the roots of Local 3, when a group of rivals came together for the better good of the people.

I hope you find this book as inspiring as I have, and that it inspires you to continue the effort toward a bright and better future for all.

ORIGINS

In the late 1800s, a small group of stationary engineers met in Chicago, Illinois, to discuss what could be done about the plight of construction and stationary workers—men with the ability to operate dangerous steam boilers—the main source of power for that time. Together they realized that without their expertise and skill, their industry could come to a standstill. But they had to organize and stand together.

On December 7, 1896, they formed the National Union of Steam Engineers of America. All but one of these men were stationary engineers; however, that would change in the coming years. When the union expanded across the border into Canada, the name was changed to the International Union of Steam Engineers.

▲ *Horse-drawn loaders and steam shovels were used for excavation at the turn of the century.*

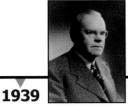

1939
IUOE convention approved creation of Local 3 in Northern California and Local 12 in Southern California.

1943
Business Manager Victor Swanson assaulted with battery acid to face. $10,000 reward offered for information.

1952
Swanson and crew board Local 3 airplane.

1958
Robert F. Kennedy led McClellan trials and brings down Swanson in corruption charges.

1960
Al Clem elected Business Manager after two years of IUOE supervision.

1969
Rancho Murieta Training Center created to begin new era in apprenticeship training and safety awareness.

As the 1900s began, the country found itself in the middle of an unprecedented building boom. Roads, dams, canals, and bridges were needed all over the nation, and these projects required men who could operate steam-driven construction equipment—men like the steam engineers of the International Union of Steam Engineers. The International began chartering union "locals" across the nation to support these men.

In California, the San Francisco earthquake of 1906 and subsequent fires caused almost total destruction, turning a vibrant city into a pile of rubble and ashes. Out of those ashes came a new and more vibrant city, with the help of the International Union of Steam Engineers.

▲ *It was a family affair using this shovel to dig a canal in 1905. (Courtesy of Dennis Moreland)*

1973

Norris Casey lost first election in close ballot after contesting and forcing second election. Dale Marr elected Business Manager in rerun election.

1982

Tom "T. J." Stapleton elected Business Manager on Green Ticket.

1996

Don Doser appointed Business Manager by officers.

1998

Rule of 85 approved and supplemental dues kept union afloat.

2003

John Bonilla appointed Business Manager by officers.

2006

Russ Burns elected Business Manager as Gold Ticket sweeps election.

15

When construction workers recognized the benefits of belonging to a union, the International Union of Steam Engineers began to see an increase in men who wanted to sign on. This meant another name change was in order. In 1912, the International Union of Steam Engineers changed its name again, becoming the International Union of Steam and Operating Engineers.

Construction workers were known as "boomers," because they generally followed an employer from one building boom project to the next, or one natural disaster to the next as was the case in 1906. But they were never assured of work and had to compete with others in the same circumstances for each and every job. The experienced man willing to work for the least amount of money generally got the job, but he always knew that there was someone waiting, standing on the sidelines, ready, willing and, in most cases, able to take his place.

One way to ensure you always got the best job was to hoard the knowledge you'd gained over years of operating your equipment. Many steam operators and firemen worked in pairs, guarding their secrets from other men who might take their jobs away. Steam was the power of the times, and this secrecy helped cut down their competition, guaranteeing them the better jobs.

▲ *Horse-drawn carriages were used to load rock and transport it down to the waiting barges at the waterfront in Richmond, California, in 1915. (Courtesy of John Fitzgerald)* Opposite Page ▶ *Workers pause for a photo with their cars and equipment at the turn of the century.*

SHUA HENDY IRON WORKS | MANUFACTURERS OF MINING & MILLING
OUNDERS - ENGINEERS - MACHINERY MERCHANTS | SAW MILLS. BOILERS STEAM ENGINES PUMPS, GAS

S G. HENES HIGH GRADE PRECISION MACHINE TOOLS
ELECTRIC CRANES - AUTOMATIC MACHINERY
ES SAN FRANCISCO AND TWIST DRILLS · REAMERS · CUTTERS AND HOBS

*"Let the workers organize. Let the toilers
assemble. Let their crystallized voice proclaim
their injustices and demand their privileges.
Let all thoughtful citizens sustain them, for
the future of labor is the future of America."*

John L. Lewis, chairman,
Committee for Industrial Organization

17

The same was also true of the men running the power shovels. A shovel runner was king among the construction workers. He demanded the highest pay and always got it. He shared his knowledge with no one. The union would someday have to deal with this issue. Guarding the keys to your own kingdom meant preventing another brother from a chance to feed and protect his family. It would take years for the unions to gain the trust of their members and loosen trade secrecy by enacting training programs. But this would come to pass.

In 1928, another name change was in order. With the advent of internal combustion engines, electric motors, hydraulic machinery, and refrigerating

Left ▲ *Operators take a break in front of the browning steam shovel.* **Right** ▲ *Steam shovels were used for excavation during the turn of the century.*

"I was trained on the job. My dad taught me welding. Work at Syar taught me skip-loader. We have to share information with others. One older member on the jobsite told me, "You're not going to have a job" if I kept sharing how-to-do info with co-workers. I told him if another worker passes me, then he deserves it. It's up to me to stay ahead of him."

Tom "T. J." Stapleton, former business manager

"They were 'boomers.' They went wherever there was work. They moved around."

Loring "Bud" Lintt, member

systems, members changed skills to keep pace with the times. The word "steam" was dropped from the union's name. It became the International Union of Operating Engineers (IUOE) and has held that name ever since.

The IUOE began chartering many small unions all over the West as operators with a variety of crafts and skill sets joined the rush to organize. By the 1930s, there were at least 14 unions chartered in California alone. Soon this would lead to a number of jurisdictional issues. Locals of the same union along with those of other crafts competed among themselves for the best jobs, undermining the importance of working together for better wages and working environments. From these early conflicts, the first leaders of Local 3 emerged.

Top ▲ Trucks waiting to be loaded at quarry in Richmond, California in 1935. Middle ▶ Chain-driven truck being loaded by this 700 P and H shovel in 1927. Bottom ▶ Northwest shovel working a quarry in Richmond, California in 1935.

Local 59, a hoisting and portable local headquartered in San Francisco, California, originally had a jurisdiction that included Alameda and Contra Costa counties all the way north to the Oregon border. Its officers were men who would become very important to the future of the Operating Engineers, not only in California, but also in the history of the IUOE: Heine Foss, president of Local 59 prior to and during the amalgamation as Local 3, Victor Swanson, Porter Vanderwark, Patrick Clancy, Frank A. Lawrence, Alton Clem, H. T. Peterson, H. O. "Curley" Spence, and Clarence Mathews.

From the minutes of these early meetings, it appears that numerous attempts were made between Local 59 and Local 45, the Steam Shovel and Dredgeman's Union, to iron out their differences. Local 45 covered all dredging in the state, as well as shovel operators and firemen on all steam rigs. Discussions hit a bottleneck in 1936 primarily over jurisdictional issues and negotiations with a group of contractors over proposed wage increases. Fines were levied against certain members of Local 45, which caused further damage to any attempts at amalgamation between the two locals.

In what was a defining moment for Swanson, a business representative, he made a plea for cooperation in a meeting held on December 31, 1936, making the following statement: "After a most complete study and investigation of all available records, it is the opinion of the signers of this report that there is little room for any disagreement between Local 45 and Local 59, and that there is absolutely no justification for this fight and turmoil between these two sister locals. It is all a costly mistake and should be rectified immediately for the common good of our members."

Opposite Page ◀ *Workers with a Bucyrus Erie tunnel mucker in 1920. (Courtesy of Al Dalton)* **Top** ▶ *Spreading black top on Highway 31 in Paisley, Oregon, 1937-1938. (Courtesy of David A. Harlan)* **Middle** ▶ *David L. Harlan taking dirt out of cut to the fill. (Courtesy of David A. Harlan)* **Bottom** ▶ *David L. Harlan moving a CAT from one area of a job to another by crossing a river. (Courtesy of David A. Harlan)*

Swanson, born in North Dakota on March 4, 1883, was a seasoned union man by 1936 having worked for the rights of union labor for many years prior to then. He tried to get the competing locals to patch things up, but his efforts only seemed to further divide them at a time when they needed to come together more than ever. He would later have his day by uniting not only these two locals but many others throughout the state. It would take more than two years from this date to accomplish that goal, but from these early records came the evidence of continued attempts that ultimately proved successful.

But things got worse before they got better. The locals were not only fighting with each other but within their own locals. These unions were run like feudal kingdoms. They were fragmented along craft lines and, as a result, it was difficult to discern whose work belonged to whom. Shovel runners out of Local 45 considered themselves a cut about the catskinners and dirt hands of locals in the area and often would have nothing to do with them—even if they were technically in the same union. They all needed to come under the same roof, under the same jurisdiction, or things would deteriorate even further.

Meanwhile, there was talk that the IUOE would issue yet another charter across the Bay in Oakland. In response, the members of Local 59 voted by a 6 to 1 margin to oppose any such charter. They would lose members and wanted none of that. On October 18, 1937, tension between the officers led to a trial and the eventual resignation of Local 59 Business Representative Frank A. Lawrence. By virtue of Lawrence's resignation, charges were withdrawn, but the damage had been done.

Soon after, on November 8, 1937, President Foss announced that, per a communication from IUOE General President John Possehl, "any members working

▲ *A steam shovel used in San Jose, California, in the 1900s. (Courtesy of Glenn Jones)*

under the jurisdiction of Local 208 should transfer to that local and make notice of his wanting a transfer in writing, to be deposited with the financial secretary." Lawrence would play a role in the formation of the newly chartered Local 208, headquartered in Oakland.

This directive created big problems for Local 59 leadership. They had to release many of their members at a time when membership was less than 400. Among the officers transferred were Peterson, Clem, and Spence. To add insult to injury, they would also have to refund application fees. The members also faced difficult economic problems, and now there was another local on the other side of the San Francisco Bay to worry about. They knew that if a man wanted to work outside his jurisdiction, either by following an employer or on

▲ *Jessie Roberts shown with steam roller from the 1920s. These were used to build roads in Palo Alto. (Courtesy of Jessie Roberts)*

his own, he would have to make sure the presiding local had no men "on the bench." If it did, he had no chance of getting the job unless he was highly skilled on a specific piece of equipment. Even then, he would have to pay a "travel fee" or "service dues" to the presiding local. To most members who used this process, it was known as paying "doby" to the new local. To many officials and business agents, the doby was theirs to keep, as they did not get much pay.

Despite the jurisdictional issues between the locals in the San Francisco Bay Area, they did stand in solidarity on larger issues. For example, in 1938, as events began to point toward World War II, the San Francisco Labor Council proposed a boycott on all Japanese goods. In response, the unions passed motions that a $25 fine be placed on members purchasing Japanese products.

In the spring of 1938, a number of special meetings were held between locals 45, 59, 59A, 59B, 842, 208, and 508 to discuss international referendums and possible merger plans. As early as May 23, 1938, the officers representing these various unions outlined a proposal for amalgamation that included the elections of officers. The plan was that these officers would manage the newly amalgamated union while under supervision of the IUOE. However, the timing wasn't right with the IUOE. Despite an election held on June 13, 1938, where Foss was elected as president, it did not happen.

In 1938, the growing use of diesel engines required engineers to become proficient in their operation in order to remain competitive. In response to this need, the IUOE president advised that ". . . all engineers who care to work at the trade learn to use the diesel engine." Inevitably, this would lead to a showdown with the Teamsters. Although early showdowns would be resolved in IUOE favor, problems with the Teamsters would persist, as would jurisdictional issues between the many unions in the Bay Area. Employers found it difficult to move their steady workers from one local's jurisdiction to another, thereby limiting the area where they could comfortably bid jobs. Compounding the problem, the IUOE continued issuing new charters for even more areas.

Something had to be done. Time was of the essence, and so on January 9, 1939, the board resolved that a delegate be sent to the 21st International Convention, less than three weeks away in Miami. At that convention, a proposal was presented to the General Executive Board to convince them to consider consolidating unions instead of creating new ones. For this reason, it was important to have representation from your home local present. The delegate selected and approved by the board was Swanson. The board also resolved that he be granted a leave of absence to attend the convention and that a temporary business representative be elected in his absence. A warrant was drawn for $750 to cover the expenses of the trip.

Swanson had his marching orders and, at the next Local 59 meeting on January 16, got further instruction from the board to "take up the question of the American Federation of Labor (AFL) and the Congress of Industrial Organizations (CIO) getting together and also about the matter concerning members carrying membership in these two different organizations." On the other side of the Bay, at Local 208, Lawrence was appointed as a delegate to the convention as well. In tandem, they pushed for consolidation of the locals in California.

In attendance at the beginning of the convention, January 23, 1939, were a number of representatives from locals in northern and southern California, but not all were present. As the convention started, discussions began with

Opposite Page ▶ Roller used on the streets of San Jose, California, in the 1900s. (Courtesy of Glenn Jones)

"*Many came out of logging and farming in the past.
They were rugged. Expected to work even if hurt.*"

Rob Wise, former officer

MADE BY
AUSTIN
MFG CO
CHICAGO

regards to California, but the final decision could not be made until two representatives, J. H. LaForce of Local 45 in San Francisco and P. A. Judd of Local 45 A in Los Angeles, arrived on the scene. Much of the discussion centered on jurisdictional issues. Whether it was the jurisdiction of production workers in oil refineries or organizing of railroad engineers, it was important to have all concerned parties present for the discussions. On Friday, January 27, 1939, the general president received a telegram from LaForce that he was leaving Los Angeles by airplane to attend the General Executive meeting and consequently the meeting was adjourned to reconvene on Monday, January 30 at 12:30 p.m.

Finally, on January 30, General President Possehl called the meeting to order with all members of the board present. LaForce and Judd (both of former steam shovel and dredgemen locals) presented the case for amalgamation of 14 local unions in California. All other representatives of the local unions of California present were informed that "No jurisdiction on building and construction work could be assured under the present existing conditions where 14 local unions of like craft jurisdiction were constantly using opportunities to trespass upon one another's territorial jurisdiction."

The union representatives of the locals in attendance were assured that "if such an understanding could be reached," they would "be cared for" and included in the setup of the new locals and they would receive salary and expenses. The local delegation was allowed time for further discussion, and the meeting was adjourned for the day. They agreed in concept to the proposal, knowing that consolidation of the unions was a progressive move, one that would establish freedom for the members to follow construction work and end the necessity for "dobying."

Possehl reviewed the situation with the General Executive Board and, after considerable discussion, directed the local and international business agents to reach agreement as to how this might be accomplished. The following day began with a call to order at 9:30 a.m. for the continuation of the General Executive Board. The representatives from California reported that they had reached an understanding and that the establishment of the two locals "with full craft and territorial jurisdiction is something they have talked about for years." In addition, they stated that establishment of two local unions in California and Nevada would allow the enactment of a universal initiation fee, dues, wages, hours, and working conditions, and a free opportunity for members to migrate throughout the two states on building and construction work with signatory employers.

With the discussion completed, the General Executive Board agreed and issued a series of resolutions to combine 14 smaller IUOE locals in California and Nevada into Local 3 and Local 12, with the two states being effectively divided in half—the northern halves being Local 3 and the southern halves Local 12. They determined that the amalgamation and transfer should be completed by February 28, 1939. Both new locals would operate under IUOE trusteeship with officers drawn largely from the administration of the former locals. LaForce, who had flown in at the last minute, was appointed as the international district representative to ensure the proper transfer and installation of Local 3.

Upon the return to the San Francisco Bay Area, the amalgamation of locals 59 and 208 was officially approved by the membership on February 6, 1939, with the other locals soon following and all coming under the fold by March 1, 1939. The General Executive Board passed a motion that every member would be notified by mail of the amalgamation of all locals in northern California and what it meant to them. Local 3 was finally a union of brothers, with jurisdiction over areas of the West, a union that would, in the next few decades, witness unprecedented growth and development.

▲ *Working an orange grove in Southern California. (Courtesy of Al Dalton)*

I n September 1939, as Hitler's march through Europe continued, Local 3 was positioned to assemble what would become the largest construction union in the United States. Its first decade began with the recently amalgamated Local 3 still under the supervision of the IUOE, but not for long. Soon after they were cut loose from international supervision, the Japanese attacked Pearl Harbor (December 7, 1941) and America entered World War II. Local 3 found itself at the forefront of an unprecedented buildup for the war effort, which would help pave the way toward a more unified, cohesive, and strong union.

The war meant jobs, and plenty of them, but it also meant that a number of recently initiated members would choose to join the military. Local 3 had more than 2,000 men enlist in the war effort, many of them going into the Navy Construction Battalion known as the Seabees.

Opposite Page ◀ Local 3 founders in Reno, Nevada, 1941. Victor Swanson (front right), Ed Doran, Mickey Murphy, Bill Waack, Heine Foss, Grover Braddack, Clarence Mathews, Harry Metz, Ses Collett, Al Clem, Pat Clancy, Joe Riley, H. T. Peterson, Curly Spence, Frank Lawrence, Jack Foster, Red Hester, Porter Vanderwark, Tom Bryson, Tom Clark (not all named). Top Left ▲ Over 2,000 Local 3 members served in World War II. Right ▶ Chain-driven steam shovels were an important piece of equipment in the early part of the 20th Century.

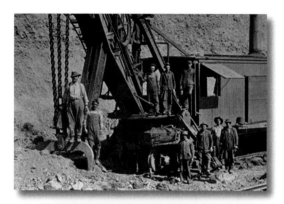

Throughout the decade, Local 3's jurisdiction grew to cover three states and the territory of Hawaii. In January 1941, Utah Local 354 joined Local 3, followed by Local 53 of Nevada in May 1943. Two years later, Utah locals 353 and 358 joined forces with Local 3 followed by Local 635 of Hawaii in August 1948.

The 1940s saw the birth of the *Engineers News*, a monthly newsletter intended to keep members "advised as to what is doing and who is doing it in the large jurisdiction of Local 3," as stated in a letter to the editor in that first issue by General IUOE President William E. Mahoney. The paper started out as an 8-page newsletter and would grow in the first few years to an invaluable 12-page newspaper, providing everything from detailed information on new union benefits, construction reports from the many districts including those in Hawaii and Utah when they came on board, employer contracts awarded, Executive Board minutes, editorials from union leaders, pin-up girls, political comics, fishing reports, and so much more.

The language and politics of the time were evident in the newspaper whether it was the "What's Doing" article from the Oakland District or the Utah "Roundup." The November 1943 issue brought the first printing of the pin-up beauties: "Just to make sure the boys in the service don't lack for pin-up beauties, we want them to have this photo of shapely Patricia Lowry of Chicago (Federated Pictures)." These pin-up girls were a regular feature throughout the war years and into the late '40s.

▲ *First issue of the* Engineers News, *March 1943.* **Opposite Page** ▶*The Robert E. Perry being christened for its maiden voyage from the Richmond, California docks on November 12, 1942.*

"We have to be involved, too much of what we depend on is determined by politics. We have to be involved."

Ken Green, member

At the local meetings and in the *Engineers News*, members were urged to buy war bonds, donate blood, and support the United Service Organizations (USO). Stories about "our boys in service" became frequent and popular additions to the newly created *Engineers News*. Men 17 to 35, who had not already received their Army induction papers, were strongly encouraged by union leaders to enlist in the Seabees. If they were catskinners, shovel runners, crane operators, or engine men, they could receive a rating of Chief Petty Officer while at the same time, practice and improve their skills.

Headlines from the
Engineers News

Stockton sets record in war bond purchases! Moved and carried that each member shall donate one days pay to the USO! Brothers and Fathers serve! Five Paine Brothers all members of Local 3 and all of them fathers of two or more children joined the service! Lend a hand, neighbor, in the biggest clearing job in the world! Be a patriot, contribute to war bonds.

Many labor issues, particularly strikes, were voluntarily suspended after America's entrance into the war and would remain so until the war was over. As stated by William Green, the president of the AFL, on a radio address: "I want to assure the American people that the American Federation of Labor is completely sincere in its no-strike pledge for the duration of the war. Until Japan surrenders, we will not excuse or condone or sanction any strike for any cause."

By adoption of a no-strike policy, the AFL reduced time lost due to strikes by its members to the lowest figure in the Federation's history. Aside from a very few local wildcat strikes, the IUOE did not authorize or approve a single strike since the bombing of Pearl Harbor. Despite a no-strike clause in the early 1940s, Local 3 did have its share of issues, the first of which was a high rate of absenteeism. Fewer workers at home meant longer hours on the job, resulting in a significant number of man-hours lost to injury, illness, or just plain fatigue. In response to this problem, the AFL officially sanctioned the 48-hour workweek as a good length, not only to help in the war effort but to cut down on absenteeism in general. To help enforce this policy, Local 3 arranged for a branch office in Richmond, at 9th and Nevin streets, to remain open until 9 p.m. on Friday nights to accommodate the membership—many of whom worked in the Richmond shipyards at that time.

Local 3's projects during the war included building temporary family units in communities all over northern California, including some of the units used to house the thousands of Japanese citizens interned by the

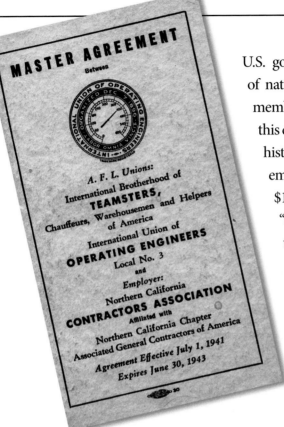

MASTER AGREEMENT

Between

INTERNATIONAL UNION OF OPERATING ENGINEERS

A. F. L. Unions:
International Brotherhood of
TEAMSTERS,
Chauffeurs, Warehousemen and Helpers
of America

International Union of
OPERATING ENGINEERS
Local No. 3
and

Employer:
Northern California
CONTRACTORS ASSOCIATION
Affiliated with
Northern California Chapter
Associated General Contractors of America

Agreement Effective July 1, 1941
Expires June 30, 1943

U.S. government for reasons of national security. Local 3 members became a part of this dark point in American history after a Local 3 employer was awarded a $1 million contract to do "a lot of new work" on the internment camp at Tule Lake. This camp was described in the *Engineers News* in 1943 regrettably as the "Jap camp."

Between 1940 and 1944, California was allotted more than $16 million in war contracts, much of it going to large-scale dredging operations. Not all of the work contracted for the war effort went smoothly. In 1943, Local 3 was involved in a battle with the CIO over units at an Army re-consignment (warehouses) site in Redding. This issue was later resolved in Local 3's favor by the National Labor Relations Board (NLRB).

Top Right ▶ *Old equipment used by charter member Bernard Hammond.*
Bottom Right ▶ *Doser with dragline in place. (Photos courtesy of Bernard Hammond)*

"We are definitely opposed to politicians who advocate quota systems. America's greatness was not built on the whiners and the criers…who will pay the taxes if the blue collar worker is left unemployed all the time?"

Al Clem, former business manager

34

$10,000 REWARD

Operating Engineers, Local Union No. 3, of the International Union of Operating Engineers, offers a reward of Ten Thousand ($10,000) Dollars, for information leading to the arrest and conviction of the individual or individuals or organization or organizations responsible for the attack upon Victor S. Swanson, Business Manager of Local No. 3, at the hour of about 10:40 P. M., December 20, 1943, on Capp Street, Near 16th Street, San Francisco, California, at which time said Victor S. Swanson was struck and acid was thrown upon his person.

All information and the identity of persons furnishing same will be kept strictly confidential, and if the informant is not required as an essential witness and he so desires, the source of the information will not be disclosed.

Persons having information shall communicate in person or by telephone with the San Francisco Police Department or any official of Local No. 3.

The Chief of Police of San Francisco, the District Attorney of San Francisco, and an official of Local No. 3 will determine who shall participate in the reward and the extent of such participation and their decision shall be final. If more than one person is entitled to the reward, it shall be proportionately distributed, the aforementioned three persons to be the sole judges of such distribution.

Dated: December 22, 1943.

Operating Engineers, Local No. 3 of the International Union of Operating Engineers

The year 1943 ended with a bang for Local 3 with what was described as a "vicious assault" on Business Manager Victor Swanson, who had been elected the previous year as an IUOE trustee. On December 20, 1943, at about 10:40 p.m., as described in reports of the day, Swanson was "slugged over the head and, as he stumbled into his automobile, the assailants threw acid over him, seriously burning his eyes, inflicting serious burns on other parts of the head, arms and chest, in addition to physical injuries resulting from the slugging." Reward posters were printed two days later. Local 3 offered the extraordinary sum of $10,000 for a reward for information leading to the arrest and conviction of the individual or individuals or organizations responsible for the attack. No one was ever apprehended.

Swanson returned to work after 78 days in the St. Francis Hospital and then, incredibly, left for the International Convention in Chicago with 11 delegates from Local 3. He would have to endure two more operations to repair damage done to his eyes. Union elections were held the next year, and the nearly blinded Swanson was reelected by a vote count of 3,238 to 623 over his competitor, George Simon. Pat Clancy ran unopposed for president, and Heine Foss was elected vice president, both with equally wide margins. As a result of his injuries, Swanson is easily recognizable in many 1940s photos as "the man in the sunglasses," which were necessary to protect his damaged eyes.

Victor Swanson

Water projects were well underway in the 1940s. One of the largest was Shasta Dam. On January 1, 1945, the last bucket of concrete was poured on the dam, leaving the giant task of moving 138 residential buildings that housed employees. With water rising behind the dam at 5,000 acre-feet a day, operators had to work quickly or risk flooding the buildings.

Opposite Page ◀ *Operators prep sewer for placement. (Courtesy of Bernard Hammond)* **Top Left** ▲ *Reward poster for attack on Business Manager Victor Swanson, December 1943.*

Also in 1945, the last of the Victory ships—the SS *Burbank*—was launched from Richmond, marking the end to an unprecedented buildup and many jobs for Local 3 members. In total, 775 ships were built in Bay Area shipyards. During this time, a group of members who worked on the ships became known as the Black Gang because they were always covered with oil and soot from the ships. The Black Gang consisted of about 70 men employed as marine oilers, firemen, and water tenders in trial crews at the various shipyards. They were the ones who tested ships before acceptance by the Maritime Commission.

In April 1945, while the nation mourned the loss of Franklin D. Roosevelt, Local 3 rallied behind his successor, Harry S. Truman, urging him to carry out the Roosevelt policies in war and peace. The end of the war was in sight, bringing great relief but also concern for union leaders. Soon, thousands of men could be returning to the job market just as the wartime projects were drying up. The AFL forecast layoffs and cutbacks. They warned

▲ *Advertisement to purchase Victory Bonds after World War II.* ▶ *International Convention held in Chicago, Illinois in April 1944. This was the first convention Local 3 officers attended as a unified local.*

· 22ND CONVENTION ·
of the INTERNATIONAL UNION OF OPERATING ENGINEERS
HOTEL STEVENS – APRIL 10-13, 1944

37

DAY SHIFT AT EUREKA DRYDOCK YARD

Here's the gang, all members of Operating Engineers, Local 3, working the day shift at the Chicago Bridge and Iron Company drydock yard at Eureka, California. Maybe you can identify some you know:

(Upper Row)—Frank Roberts, A. L. McCool, F. D. Brown, Winton Edgman, Andy Anderson, Larry Johnson, Jack Thompson, Ernie Sundquist, Herb Joppan, Roy Stevens, Charlie Lakin, Russell Griffin, Varil Nims, Jim Pastori, John Mosely, Frank Loveland, Chet Dryden, Bill Hoxie, Eugene Burrill, Jack Niskey, Harley Helm, John Mitts, Charley Lewis, Elmer Hodkinson, Lloyd Bailey.

(Center Row)—John Cain, Fred Domenighini, Archie Dahl, Ed Miller, Frank Tehan, Sam Hoskins, Tom Hitchings, Harry Johnson, Roscoe Miller, Vic Raymond, Norm Beck, John Threadgill, Roston Dillard, Rico Pastori (seated), Walter Hansen, Oscar Johansen, Hans Jorgensen, Jack Howard (seated), S. A. Gouthier, Sam Amigo, Art Stewart, Ellis Smith.

(Lower Row)—C. R. Bernard, John Bullack, Lou Owens, M. W. Edwards, Charles Petersen, Bill Kuchel, Jos. M. Saraiva, Darrell Betts, Jess Van Cleave, Pat Furnish, Bill Goetz, Wm. Olsen, Byron Fassett, W. Warren, Hans Salstrom, Arts Santelli, James Earl, Robt. Mor..., John Lema, Walter Stanbrough.

ENGINEERS LOCAL 3 A. F. of L. OCT-NOV-DEC 1943

'Teen-age ball team by Engineers, a bang-up

During the past season these boys have chalked up a very nice record for themselves—14 games won, 7 lost and 2 tied. On Sunday, September 23, the club was invited to play at Yont-

ville before a group of Veterans of Foreign Wars, and at this game won their first trophy.

At the present time plans are being made to enter the team in the Eagles East Oakland winter league. Play in this league will start about the middle of October and if the plans are carried out we will publish a schedule of games in our November issue.

These kids really play a bang-up game of ball and we would like to have more of you members turn out in support of them.

NEIGHBOR—O... favor of th... policy is... a native... She is he... "Today... Perklna...

ENGINEERS LOCAL 3 A. F. of L. JAN-FEB-MAR 1946

*Top ▲ Eureka Drydock group shot. **Middle** ▲ Pin up girls were a regular feature in the news. **Bottom** ▲ Local youth baseball teams were often sponsored by Local 3. **Right** ▶ Clementine Dam under construction on the north fork of the American River. (Courtesy of Marvin Reed) **Opposite Page** ▶ Barge preparing materials in quarry project. (Courtesy of Bernard Hammond)*

Congress that health and job problems would persist if the nation was not prepared for a return to full employment, suggesting that an extension of Social Security benefits might guard against the hazards.

As the so-called "Problems of Peace" were debated, suddenly they became less hypothetical. The Soviet Union formally declared war on Japan. Their entrance into the war, followed by the dropping of the atomic bomb, brought a dramatic and sudden end to war and left the country on "pins and needles" as Japan stalled on acceptance of the final surrender terms.

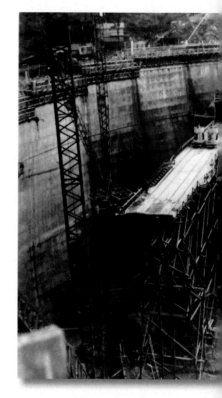

Realizing that final surrender meant the job market would soon be flooded with new workers, the Labor-Management Charter (to aid postwar recovery) was signed. This charter promised high wages and full employment for maximum postwar production. It also recognized labor's right to organize and collectively bargain. Meanwhile, in the U.S. Senate, talks began to reduce the workweek from 48 to 40 hours. In California, on September 5, 1945, the California Highway Commission in Sacramento allocated funds for the construction of a large number of projects totaling more than $49 million, adding to the list of postwar infrastructure projects.

There is still the pride in craftsmanship in what they do. The only way we are going to compete with non-union is to out-produce them."

Bill Burns, former officer

As soon as the troops began returning from the war, looking for homes and jobs, the AFL began immediate work on a number of overdue items, including support for the shorter workweek. The shorter workweek, they asserted, "will spread available employment and give the nation's workers and their families the opportunity for healthful recreation and education, which our modern civilization affords."

The AFL also began what it called the "greatest organizing drive in the history of unionism," setting a goal of 1 million new members. In the West, the effort to organize the oil and steel industries began in northern California with the Operating Engineers' first charter at Standard Oil Local 21 in Richmond. The effort quickly spread to Utah, where non-union firms, under contract to a Utah oil refining company, started moving in to build pipelines, among other things.

Catching the spirit of the times, on the front page of the February 16, 1945, issue of the *Engineers News*, Henry J. Kaiser, owner of the Henry J. Kaiser Company, made an appeal to "begin talks about what we hoped for after the war, for a west and south competing on equal terms not only for a share of America's wealth but for a part in her progress . . . It is enlightened self-interest—it is World Peace."

Top ◀ *Mixer trucks in the 1940s. (Courtesy of Igor Blake)* *Bottom* ◀ *Paul Muck working a grader. (Courtesy of Gerald Muck)*

Now that workers had returned home, the mining industry began heating up and this meant more members for Local 3. In April 1945, despite a few complications, Utah's Local 353 in the copper industry prepared to become part of Local 3. In August 1945, after other bidders dropped out, Kaiser made a bid to purchase Geneva Steel. This was good news for Local 3 as Kaiser intended to operate Geneva Steel in connection with his California plant in Fontana.

In the following year, Local 3 would make news of a different sort by becoming the first union in the United States to own its own plane, piloted by none other than Local 3's Clancy. The plane would ultimately meet its demise at the end of the runway in the early '50s, but it helped the Local 3 staff reach the growing jurisdiction quickly. Unfortunately, airplanes and other perceived excesses on the part of the unions would lead to the passage of the Taft-Hartley law in 1947, a law that among other things outlawed closed shops and required unions to notify owners of pending strikes. Local 3 waged an all-out call to President Truman to veto this law, but his veto was overridden in the Republican-dominated senate.

The year 1948 was a year of dredge, power, and road projects, including the beginning of a 25-year dredge program with a large project on the Yuba River to dig a 600-foot channel to a depth of 126 feet. Local 3's influence continued to grow at the state level when Frank Lawrence, who played a part in the early development of Local 3, was elected president of the California State Building Trades Council at a special meeting of the council's executive board on September 11.

Toward the end of the 1940s, innovation was booming, especially for operating engineers. "The First Real Modern Project," so-called by Local 3 Business Representative M. B. "Mickey" Murphy, was a project in Monterey Bay at the breakwater across to Moss Landing for Pacific Gas and

▲ *The February 16, 1945 edition of* Engineers News. ▶ *Diving heavy duty mechanics wage scales in the mid 1940s.*

Electric (PG&E), done with a "real modern" piece of equipment. Real modern in those days was a Koehring Truck Crane, complete with a radio, an electric coffee maker, and an electric shaver. Murphy reported, "You can shave at 7:30, have coffee at 10, and get news all day long!" The proud operator of this "Modern Miracle" was James Brown, assisted by oiler Harold Malcolm.

On August 7, 1948, Hawaii became a part of Local 3's jurisdiction. In 1941, the territory was issued a charter (Local 635, Honolulu) by the IUOE with a jurisdiction including the Hawaiian and Pacific islands. Located at 214 McCandless in Honolulu, J. K. Waiwaiole, a former representative of Local 635, was put in charge of an office with lots of things to be straightened out. Because many of the contractors came from the States, and Hawaii was still only a territory, they realized that much of the work of union organizing would have to be done in the States, and it would be easier to do if a part of Local 3. To organize contractors in California meant that when they came to Hawaii or the Pacific Islands, they would be part of the union already and could easily be brought into the fold within Local 3's jurisdiction.

In the fall elections of 1948, a key issue was a major water reclamation bill pending in Congress. This bill would ensure funding for the Folsom Dam project, a project estimated to last about three years and employ between 1,000 and 2,000 members. However, on October 2, 1948, as assembled dignitaries heard the first blast symbolizing the beginning of construction on the dam, the future of the project was uncertain. The bill had still not passed Congress. Local 3 would have to wait until the end of 1948, when the bill passed, signifying that Congress had put the West firmly on the path toward the necessary postwar expansion of power, water, and flood control projects long needed and deserved. Water reclamation projects have always been vital to the state of California where the climate fluctuates regularly from drought to flood as its population booms.

Have a blast this Holiday season From the gang at ... ... Quarry Products, Inc.

▲ *Quarry Products Postcard. (Courtesy of John Fitzgerald)*

Throughout the '40s and into the '50s, dynamite blasts, such as those used at Folsom Dam, were a common way to break up rock, and a science all to itself. Tunneling into the rocky soil was no easy task. In addition, the size of the numerous charges had to be calculated and at what stages the explosions would be set in order to get the mountain rock to fall into place. Fewer and fewer people knew this science, and as a result, blasting with dynamite was eventually outlawed altogether except for a few companies that had proven knowledge, engineering, and a history. One such company was Blake Brothers in Richmond, which continued to dig tunnels, set charges, and bring down mountains with blasts of up to 40 tons into the 1950s.

A number of employers have spanned the 70-year history of Local 3, but not many date back to a founding in 1904. The Blake Brothers Company, founded in 1904, was an asphalt and paving company that had roots going back even further to a company called the Oakland Paving Company. The company has employed many unions, but the Operating Engineers was there early on to run the Osgood shovels and other heavy equipment used to move rock. In 1963, Blake Brothers sold the quarry and surrounding land, but the quarry and its union contracts are still in place with the current employer.

---

work day. On repair work, eight (8) hours work between the hours of 8:00 o'clock a.m. and 4:30 o'clock p.m. shall constitute a work day. All time worked in excess of eight (8) hours, and all time worked on Saturdays, Sundays and Holidays shall be paid for at the rate of time and one-half (1½) except when dredge is operated on Sundays and Holidays, the members of the crew engaged in its operation shall be paid at double time rate. The full crew employed in the operation of a dredge shall all commence work at the dsignated starting time of shift.

On three (3) shift operations, the straight time hours shall be from 12:01 a.m. Monday to Midnight Friday.

On two shift operations, the straight time hours shall be from 8:00 a.m. to 12:00 Midnight.

When more than one shift is worked, shifts shall run consecutively.

The following days shall be considered legal holidays: New Year's Day, Memorial Day, Fourth of July, Labor Day, Thanksgiving Day and Christmas Day. The fraction of a day shall be paid for as a whole day if the employee reports to work at the regular starting time. Any employee who quits before completing his day's work shall be paid for the actual time worked. The fraction of one hour to be paid for as one hour.

However, it is understood that the starting time on single shift jobs shall not be changed except by a mutual agreement between the Employer and the Union, and in such case it will only be changed because of conditions which create the necessity for a change of starting time.

—3—

5. **WAGES**
Hydraulic Suction Dredges

	Straight Time
Chief Engineer	$400.00 per mo.
Leverman	1.90 per hour
Assistant Engineer (Steam or Electric)	1.65 per hour
Welder	1.65 per hour
Fireman or Oiler	1.30 per hour
Deckmate	1.50 per hour
Levee Foreman	1.50 per hour
Leveeman	1.30 per hour
Deckhand (can operate anchor scow under direction of deckmate)	1.30 per hour

Clam-Shell Dredges

Leverman	1.90 per hour
Deckmate	1.50 per hour
Deckhand	1.30 per hour
Fireman or Oiler	1.30 per hour
Watch Engineer	1.65 per hour
Barge Mate (Seagoing)	1.50 per hour
Bargeman	1.30 per hour

6. When the employer transfers the employees from dock to dredge and/or from dredge to dock; when employees are going to work or returning therefrom, it is agreed that should the time taken in transfer in either direction exceed twenty (20) minutes, the Employer shall pay to each employee being transferred the sum of $0.50 for each fifteen (15) minutes or fraction thereof that the transfer time exceeds twenty (20) minutes.

7. Where a higher rate of wages is being paid herein stipulated, nothing in this agreement shall be construed as lowering such wages.

8. All men shall be allowed a meal period of thirty (30) minutes during the fourth

—4—

43

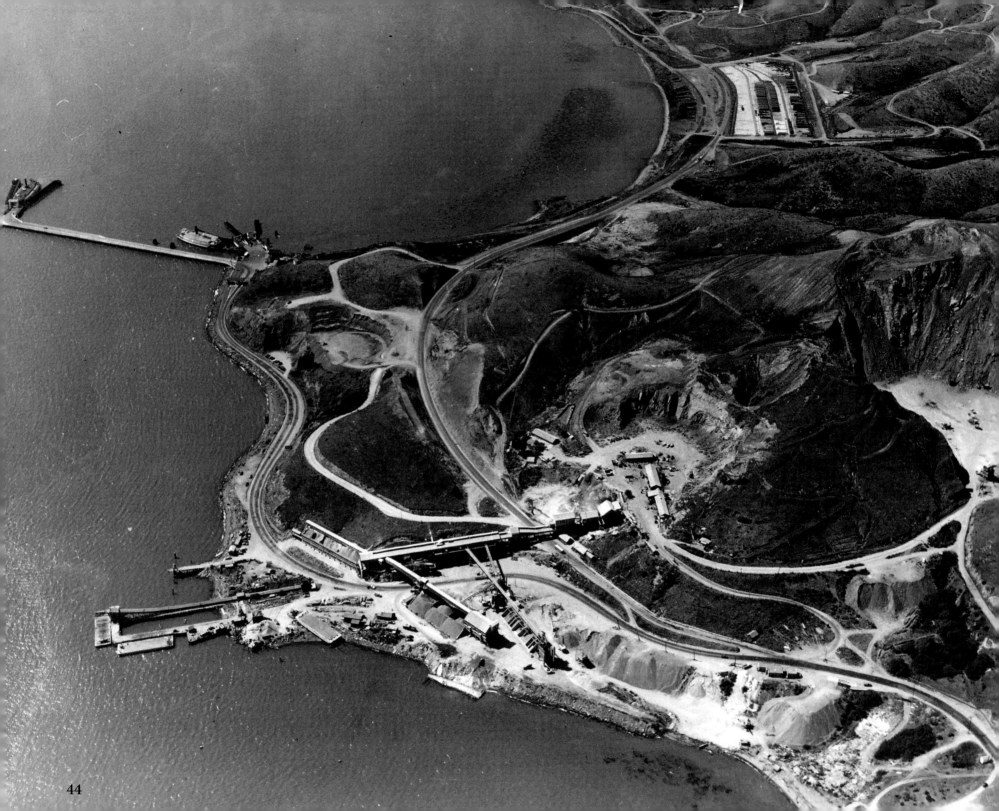

As the 1940s ended, California was hit with "The Big Freeze of '49," the worst weather in 15 years. As a result, work on several big projects ground to a halt. Dredgers and catskinners were forced to wait for Mother Nature to have mercy on them. Finally the spring thaw began, and they were able to get to work on several big projects.

As always, union leaders seized every opportunity to organize catskinners, shovel operators, and engineers. "I'm looking toward the time when those boys will all be wearing a 'Big 3' button on the side of their hat," said Eureka Business Representative Otto E. Never, after Hawkins Logging Company signed the union agreement.

Local 3's first decade was not easy, but incredible progress had been made and its members had reason to be proud. They had paved the way for an era of postwar growth in the West and Hawaii, which would give them power beyond what the early founders could have possibly foreseen, power that would lead to internal conflicts in the decade to come.

Opposite Page ◀ *An aerial of a quarry being worked by the Blake Brothers Company in the 1940s.* **Above left** ▲ *Anson Blake in his office in 1948.* **Top Right** ▶ *A barge used by Blake Brothers Company.* **Bottom Right** ▶ *Blake Brothers Quarry Asphalt Ready Mix Operation in 1947. (Photos courtesy of Igor Blake)*

B y the 1950s, the hard work of setting up Local 3 and establishing it as an important player in the growth of the West had been done; however, what lay ahead was the equally hard work of keeping it going through the Korean War and the many internal struggles that followed.

On June 25, 1950, the United States, under the auspices of the United Nations, joined other allies to defend South Korea from aggressions from the north. As hostilities increased, Communist China and Russia threw their mighty weight behind North Korea, causing concerns among our allies that the United States would be tempted to drop another atomic bomb. So began a chilly period of uncertainty called "the cold war."

the NEW INTERNATIONAL TD-24

THE NEW INTERNATIONAL TD-24 140 DRAWBAR HORSEPOWER DIESEL CRAWLER

This equipment will be on display and demonstrated at the Bay Cities Equipment Co., 28th & Cypress, Oakland, on April 22. Operators, Superintendents and Mechanics are invited to attend the showing, starting at 9 a.m. (Luncheon served.)

Issues surrounding the war economy would dominate the early 1950s. Unions saw Congress-enacted Manpower acts, which were intended to mobilize the workforce for defense, as "manpower grabs." Their view was that government and big business were using the Korean War as an excuse to drive up prices while keeping wages down and demonizing the unions. In an attempt to debug the "Big Business Fables" about the unions being spread by the government, the *Engineers News* began publishing a monthly series called "Your Economics and Mine," distributed by the California State Federation of Labor. It was the beginning of a struggle between the unions and big business, which would lead to both internal and external political problems in the late '50s.

However, the early 1950s were also a very patriotic time for Local 3. Many members joined the war effort as "Combat Engineers" and stories were printed in the news about the heroes, their bravery, those missing in action, and those who had given the ultimate sacrifice.

Opposite Page◄ Ponderay Lake, Idaho, in 1953 with a HD 21 tractor in background. From left: Chuck Trisdale, Jack Tucker (mechanic), Bradford (government inspector), Kris Kristopherson (sub-contractor), Talbert (government inspector), Grafton (resident engineeer), Floyd Leonard, unknown mechanic, Al Pores (sub-contractor), Ward Allen, John Trisdale (general contractor), George Nelson (general superintendent of J.H. Trisdale Inc.), Charlie Freesh (sub-contractor), and Bob Lohoff (pilot for J.H. Trisdale Inc.) (Courtesy of Bob Leslie) ▲ In the early years, employers and equipment manufactures had advertisements in the Engineers News.

On the home front, the passage of Taft-Hartley in 1947 signaled the need to create some sort of fund to legally fight anti-union threats. And so, in September 1950, Local 3 created a Defense Fund. Union officers decided that money set aside in this fund would be handled differently from other union funds. No warrants would be needed to remove money, and no bills kept to show how money was dispersed.

Having such a fund would ultimately lead to charges of impropriety. The most scathing charges would come from a group of members who kept their identities a secret, publishing a newsletter called the *Construction Stiffs News*. The stiffs complained about the size of the union, the agreements with contractors, and the questionable acts of certain union officials. These stiffs would ultimately help bring about the downfall of Victor Swanson. He became determined to expose their "sneaky and cowardly behavior" by whatever means at his disposal. In 1957, this obsession would backfire disastrously for both him and Local 3.

▲ *Leo Wendt in 1958. (This photo and photo on opposite page courtesy of Joe Wendt)*

While these issues percolated at union headquarters, union members were busy working on some mighty big projects. For example, in 1951, Congress authorized $1 billion for defense housing, the East Bay Municipal Utility Department prepared to build a giant sewage disposal plant, and highway work was in full swing all over the San Francisco Bay Area, Nevada, and Utah. In Hawaii, which was not yet a state, work was set to begin on a naval air station in Kaneohe.

In 1952, Harry S. Truman, whose popularity had dropped to an all-time low, was retiring from the political arena. Illinois Governor Adlai Stevenson, who was pro-union, was the new Democratic nominee. His Republican opponent was General Dwight D. Eisenhower, who had supported Taft-Hartley and the anti-union Right-to-Work referendums that several states were set to vote on.

"I was involved in a campaign at San Francisco Chemical versus the UMV. When we went out for house calls, we actually were visiting people living in tents on the hillsides. No amenities. No sanitation."

Tom "T. J." Stapleton, former business manager

Business Manager Victor Swanson (far left) and crew on the wing of the Local 3 airplane.

As the election neared, the unions launched an unprecedented campaign in support of pro-union candidates and against Right-to-Work. Editorials condemning Right-to-Work appeared every month in the *Engineers News* along with special pleas from union officers to get out the vote: "Call everyone on your Christmas list," they urged, "Right-to-Work will destroy every type of union security." Many in the unions did not yet know the power of their vote. As Swanson commented, "Our enemies know our potential far better than we do."

Labor was such a hot topic in 1952 that the *Wall Street Journal* reported "...the influx of the labor press could be a potent factor in determining the voting results . . ." because of "the rank-and-file discontent with wage stabilization and with rising living costs." However, despite the all-out campaign, Eisenhower was elected president in November, and Nevada voted for Right-to-Work. Bitterly disappointed, Local 3 nonetheless pledged "to the incoming president of the United States our full support as patriotic Americans." This pledge of support to the new president wouldn't last too long.

The next year, 1953, the union fought many battles to improve health and welfare benefits. These battles led to frequent lockouts by the Associated General Contractors (AGC). The union cited the AGC's "stubborn attitude" and its desire to "use part of the welfare funds for payments to the trustees and for paying of huge fees to a high-priced consultant whom they have brought into the picture entirely of their own initiative" as the reasons for the lockouts. Finally, after five long

months of lockouts and disputes, in August, the union and AGC agreed to enter into a period of arbitration. It would take more than 25 meetings and last into the next year but eventually they would come up with a plan.

The union also fought in Sacramento to improve disability insurance and jobless benefits that were "shamelessly low." However, in this battle they would face an unlikely foe, the powerful California Medical Association (CMA). The CMA's unethical opposition to raising disability benefits would help defeat legislation beneficial to the working man and cause union leaders to mourn the loss of the "old family doctor."

In July 1953, hostilities in Korea ceased with neither side declaring victory. As had happened after World War II, the unions sounded the alarm about the consequences of the sudden loss of military jobs, coupled with rising prices. Their influence would lead to congressional actions to stabilize wages while holding down prices.

▲ *Trench work at Corte Madera in 1952. (Courtesy of Harold Puckeylow)* ▲

"Employees are hard to unify, but it can be done with constant education regarding the issues that affect them. Have to overcome cultural barriers that prevent them from standing together as a union."

Harold Lewis, former officer

NOV. 19. 1952
LAST LOAD OF EARTH

KAJAKAI DAM

AFGHANISTAN

The labor movement finally got some "Ivy League" respect in 1954. In June, Harvard University offered its first course on "Trade Unions," an acknowledgement from the country's premier university of the contributions of labor to America's growth and strength. Local 3 has supported this program since its inception and continues sending key staff members to this day.

The AGC's Health and Welfare plan, a major issue from the previous year, would finally be released in 1954. In March, the complete plan was printed in the *Engineers News* along with a sample registration form. An analysis of the plan, titled "Umpire's Decision and Opinion on the Health Plan," was also published. Some of the benefits had been compromised but union leaders still urged members to sign up. This plan would continue to change and improve over the coming decades.

Opposite Page ◀ *Brother Roy Kingery and crew in Afghanistan as the last load of dirt is emptied for Kajakai Dam, November 19, 1952. (Courtesy of Roy Kingery)* **Left** ▲ *Work on Bayshore Freeway in 1959.* **Middle** ▲ *Benicia Ferry in 1960.* **Right** ▲ *Work on the Berkeley Sewer in the 1950s. (Photos on this page courtesy of Bernard Hammond)*

Meanwhile, engineers were hard at work on projects such as Folsom Dam, Honolulu Airport, Reno Airport, the Bay Bridge approach known as the Cypress Structure, and many highway projects all over Local 3's jurisdiction. There were still some skirmishes reported, particularly with the Teamsters, whose "astonishing" raids on Local 3 projects never seemed to stop.

In the state elections of 1954, Local 3 participated in another massive get-out-the-vote campaign for pro-labor candidates and platforms. In California, the effort was successful and a pro-union Democratic governor was voted in; however, in Nevada, the attempt to repeal Right-to-Work was defeated. After the elections, California Governor Goodwin Knight appointed former Local 3 officer Frank Lawrence as the state industrial accident commissioner. Lawrence's influence in state politics continued to grow as he urged all members to report industrial accidents no matter how small, as quickly as possible. Industrial safety would become a major issue for decades to come.

▼ *Dredging of Prospect Slough in the 1960s. (Courtesy of Al Dalton)*

The year 1955 started out fortuitously. In February, Swanson was elected president to the San Francisco Public Utilities Commission, a powerful commission that oversaw the Water Department, San Francisco Municipal Railway (Muni), San Francisco Airport, and the Hetch Hetchy project. The purpose of the commission was to ensure that consumers have safe, reliable utility service at reasonable rates. A few months later, the AFL and the CIO decided to end a 20-year split in organized labor, resolving to create a new organization called the AFL-CIO. This move was applauded by organized labor but was little help in the struggle against anti-union referendums. In March, Utah would join Nevada as a Right-to-Work state.

In the midst of a housing project boom later that summer, Local 3 again clashed with the AGC. The dispute was over wages that hadn't increased despite the demand for more and more housing, and caused a serious walkout. As he had in the past, Swanson arbitrated the dispute, gaining the members a $0.125-per-hour increase in wages.

The year 1955 ended tragically for many in Local 3's jurisdiction. A major flood, described aptly as "an evil stranger of Christmas Eve," ravaged much of northern California, killing more than 100 people and causing more than $200 million in damage. The tragedy could have been even worse, were it not for the Shasta Dam, completed in mid-1945 by the Operating Engineers. It was credited with saving the cities of Redding and Red Bluff. On the other hand, delays on building the Coyote Dam were blamed for much "ruin and death."

The next year, Local 3 stepped up to the plate and did its part to help restore and repair what had been damaged. In January 1956, in response to devastating Christmas Eve floods, a $2 million water control project was announced in Sacramento. This, along with reports of flood damage and repair projects, would dominate the minds of Local 3 officials until at least March when politics, both national and internal, again took center stage.

In national politics, Eisenhower was up for reelection. As they had in the past, unions planned massive get-out-the-vote campaigns to unseat him and other Republicans who had "done nothing for the little people of America. They (the Republicans) openly catered to the wealthy in give-away contracts and tax relief while ignoring the urgent plea to relieve the tax burden of American workers."

Meanwhile, at the International Convention, IUOE Vice President Swanson went on record as being opposed to the so-called "international agreements" supported by IUOE General President William E. Mahoney. Swanson was

▶ *Treasure Island dolphin piles in the 1950s.*
  (Courtesy of Bernard Hammond)

particularly opposed to the railroad and pipeline agreements. He felt that these agreements would lead to wages and working conditions that were "lesser" than those negotiated locally. This disagreement with President Mahoney would lead to a falling out between the two men. Swanson would later challenge Mahoney's position as the general president. Mahoney and his predecessor, General President John Possehl, had begun to think that Local 3 had too much power, referring to it as the West Coast International. This power struggle would not end in Swanson's favor.

Back home, there were many big projects in 1956 that kept Local 3 members off the bench, including a $50 million rail fill job in Salt Lake City, military housing in Oahu, big tunnel projects in Marysville, California, and the completion of the Richmond/San Rafael Bridge.

In the latter part of 1956, union officials began focusing their attention not only on health and safety issues but also on complaints of discrimination, particularly against older workers.

▲ *Swanson and crew posing on a new piece of equipment in the early 1950s. (Courtesy of Russ Swanson)*

In September, in response to discrimination claims, the U.S. Department of Labor launched a comprehensive study of hiring policies and the work potential of "oldsters." At that time, an "oldster" was anyone over 40.

In November 1956, the *Engineers News* published an article titled "Chemicals in Food that May Cause Cancer," which was ahead of its time. The article was a reprint from a report published after an international "union against cancer" meeting in Switzerland. It stated that ". . . a number of food additives used in the U.S. and elsewhere as dyes, thickeners, sweeteners and preservatives are cancer-producing." The U.S. Consumer's Union dismissed this claim, saying that there was "nothing essentially wrong" with chemicals used in food. Of course, we know now that they were wrong, demonstrating how Local 3 was ahead of its time in the health and welfare of its membership.

The next month, the *Engineers News* published an article from the National Research Council entitled "Noise can kill." This article focused on the critical need for noise-suppression equipment at certain work sites. Many operators suffered hearing damage, rendering some with little-to-no hearing after working on noisy jobsites. However, new technology in noise suppression was just around the corner, and Local 3 was ready, willing, and able to jump on the bandwagon.

Nineteen fifty-seven would be a year that members of Local 3 would not soon forget. In January, Congress appointed a bipartisan committee called the Select Committee on Improper Activities in the Labor or Management Field (or the McClellan Committee) to "study the extent of criminal or other improper practices in the field of labor-management relations or in groups of employees or employers." They began a series of investigations that lasted until 1960 and resulted in the enactment of the Labor-Management Reporting and Disclosure Act.

Later that same year, Swanson was implicated in scandals that would put Local 3 squarely under the McClellan Committee's radar. The first was a suspicious land deal in Stockton that landed him in hot water with the IUOE. The second was a bungled scheme to find out who was writing the "slander-filled" *Construction Stiffs News* by hiring an ex-convict and paying him in cash from the Defense Fund. This got the attention of the FBI.

▲ *The Caterpillar Diesel Twin D8 with a brush rake cleared land of all trees and brush for the reservoir behind the Hungry Horse Dam. This dam is on the south fork of the Flathead River in northern Montana, a few miles south of Glacier National Park.* **Opposite Page** ▶ *John Trisdale in the operator's seat of the Caterpillar Diesel Twin D8 Tractor at the Hungry House Project in Montana. (Photos courtesy of Bob Leslie)*

"To organize, you have to go to the guy's home, meet his wife and kids – that makes the difference. The wife wants security for her kids and to have health care."

Tom "T. J." Stapleton, former business manager

"I walked up to the two catskinners and said, 'I know it's steep and I don't want you hurt, but there's a certain way you do steep country and there's a way you don't. We gotta clear it, there ain't no such thing as can't. I was in an Army unit in Korea that was named 'Can Do.' I said there ain't no such thing as 'can't.' You can do anything with this equipment if you do it the right way. .."

Manuel Spessard, member

In June 1957, Swanson was forced to take a three-month leave of absence to fight both of these charges. IUOE President Mahoney selected Newell J. Carman to take over, saying in a letter to Local 3, "Swanson has, and some of his other officers and representatives may have violated the Ritual, Obligation, Laws, Rules and Decisions of the Organization and the Constitution of the IUOE." President Mahoney also announced that Local 3 was being placed under the supervision of the International Union.

In January 1958, the McClellan Committee questioned members of the IUOE in Washington DC. They began by stating that an investigation of the IUOE was crucial. After all, the Operating Engineers were "the backbone of a $40 billion federal road-building program . . ." and a "vital requirement in the construction of bridges, tunnels, oil wells, pipelines, factories, airports, and every other major building project in this country."

The Commission accused the IUOE of operating like an "exclusive club" where it was "imperative a member maintain membership in order to get a job." General President Mahoney was subpoenaed

---

Opposite Page ◄ *Early equipment at what would become the Rancho Murieta Training Center in the late 1960s.*

McClellan Committee & Trials

The McClellan Committee consisted of: Sen. John L. McClellan Chairman, Sens: Irving Ives, J.F. Kennedy, Sam J. Erwin, Jr., Pat McNamara, Barry Goldwater, Karl E. Mundt. Chief counsel: R. F. Kennedy, Investigator: Pierre Salinger

In total, the McClellan Commission conducted 253 active investigations, served 8,000 subpoenas for witnesses and documents, held 270 days of hearings with 1,526 witnesses (343 of whom invoked the Fifth Amendment), compiled almost 150,000 pages of testimony.

The final report of the committee was issued on March 31, 1960. After the report was issued, the Senate transferred their authority to the Committee on Government Operations.

From McClellan trials:

Senator Curtis: What was the reason that all these people working belonged to your union?

Mr. Clancy: They joined like any other good American citizen, the working man. They joined to better their hours and working conditions, which they have done in the State of California."

In February, President Mahoney, who had been too ill to attend the McClellan trials, resigned and Joseph Delaney was named IUOE president.

In Washington the findings of the McClellan commission had led to the enactment of the Labor-Management Reporting and Disclosure Act (Public Law 86-257) on September 14, 1959. This act provided member rights, legitimate trusteeship and performance standards by union officials. The Department of Labor was designated as investigative agency for member complaints.

to appear before the McClellan Committee, but he was in a Miami hospital. He did not appear before the committee, stating that under the advice of his doctor he was forced to resign his office.

Local 3 Business Manager Victor Swanson and representative Pat Clancy were brought before the committee. They passionately defended the value of the unions for the working man and denied using any strong-arm tactics. Swanson swore under oath: "Senator McClellan, you can take every drop of my blood and you will not find one drop for a dictatorship. You won't find one drop."

In California, the McClellan Commission investigation resulted in Proposition 18—a proposition put before the voters that was known as the "Employer-Employee Relations" or "Open Shop" proposal. It was scorned by unions as "a threat to every segment of the population," because it would create "an unlimited, no holds-barred competition for work. Jobs are given to the lowest bidder, someone who wouldn't dare ask for overtime money."

Despite the political upheaval of 1958, two large-scale projects began: Trinity Dam, which would employ 500 engineers, and the $7 million Olympics project at Squaw Valley.

In 1959, Local 3 made significant improvements in communications, safety, and retirement assistance. In January, the Federal Communications Commission (FCC) granted Local 3 a license to operate its own shortwave radio network. The so-called "Radio Net" allowed union officials to communicate with men working in remote areas, such as highway projects and dams. Radio Net allowed those men not only to communicate with Local 3 headquarters but also with members at other sites.

Later that year, a fatal tunnel accident at the Oroville Dam again underscored the need for safety on construction jobs. In response, Carman, the man put in charge by the IUOE as a result of the McClellan trials, established a safety program to ensure that "No matter what type of work you are doing, or where you are doing it, observe, correct, and report all unsafe conditions and keep an eye open . . ." This program will continue in the next couple of decades.

The year 1959 also saw at least one major labor dispute. This dispute, at the Kennecott operation in Bingham Canyon, Utah, was an alleged Taft-Hartley violation that went before the NLRB. A special election was held at the plant, with the workers voting 2 to 1 in favor of Local 3. As a result, many non-union workers opted to join.

Another topic on the minds of the common man in the 1950s was retirement. In 1959, the Pension Trust Fund was launched with employer contributions of 5 cents per hour. However setting up the pensions would take a long time because, without computers, individual records had to be manually created for each member of Local 3. By 1963, employer contributions were 15 cents an hour and in 1964, they were raised to 20 cents an hour in the northern California construction industry.

After a tumultuous decade, fraught with strife, the 1950s ended, appropriately, with a bang. As the new state of Hawaii celebrated its admission into the United States as the 50th state, the Mauna Loa Volcano exploded, thrilling the islanders, one of whom wrote: "Words cannot be found to fully describe the beauty of this fiery fountain of molten rock which at times has spouted to heights of 1,700 feet!" It was a fitting ending to a year of internal struggle.

I n the 1960s, turbulent political and social issues dominated the mainstream news; however, for Local 3, this was a decade of unprecedented growth in both membership and organizational strength. The decade would end on an exhilarating note as the first American astronaut walked on the moon in front of millions of TV viewers. The growth of technology that enabled this feat would not have been possible without operating engineers.

Throughout the previous decade, Local 3 had battled the anti-union policies of the administration in power, calling on its members to unite against Right-to-Work initiatives, for the repeal of Taft-Hartley, and against Republican candidates running for office. Not surprisingly, given Robert F. Kennedy's aggressive interrogation of union officials during the McClellan trials, there was little attention paid to his brother John's victory in 1960. However, Democratic presidents had proven supportive of the unions in the past and so, soon after the presidential election, Local 3's focus turned toward improving on-the-job safety, providing training programs, and helping members achieve more financial security. The fiery political rhetoric of the previous decade had died down.

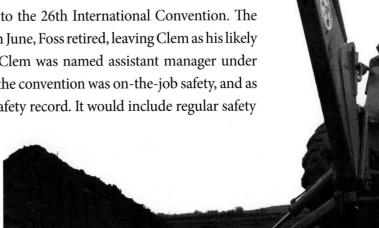

The decade opened with the election of delegates to the 26th International Convention. The leading vote-getters were Heine Foss and Al Clem. In June, Foss retired, leaving Clem as his likely successor and, accordingly, the following month, Clem was named assistant manager under IUOE Supervisor Newell Carman. The key issue at the convention was on-the-job safety, and as a result, Clem created a plan to improve Local 3's safety record. It would include regular safety meetings, awards, and an increased effort to get out the word through the *Engineers News*.

Opposite Page ◄ *Graduation ceremony at Camp Roberts with Local 3 and Local 12 graduates in attendance with their officers.*

26th International Union of Operating Engineers Convention, Americana Hotel in Bal Harbour, Florida, April 11-15, 1960.

MOBILE L.U. 653

ATLANTA L.U. 926

BIRMINGHAM L.U. 312

"If you look at the labor movement across the nation, Local 3 always had some of the best leadership in the nation."

Bill Burns, former officer

Local 3's Safety Plan recognized that on-the-job safety was dependent on certain key ingredients. Members had to be properly trained on equipment, which in turn had to be properly maintained. In addition, employers had to be vigilant and ensure that their employees were not over-worked or asked to perform tasks they were not trained to do.

The *Engineers News* ran numerous cartoons and editorials calling on members to follow all safety procedures and report any unsafe conditions. Current legislation (Foran's Bill) out of Sacramento provided that any employer found guilty of violating safety regulations could be fined, but the violation had to be reported first.

Al Clem
Business Manager 1960-1973

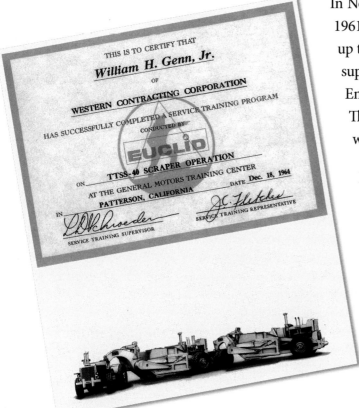

THIS IS TO CERTIFY THAT

William H. Genn, Jr.

OF

WESTERN CONTRACTING CORPORATION

HAS SUCCESSFULLY COMPLETED A SERVICE TRAINING PROGRAM

CONDUCTED BY

EUCLID

ON **TTSS-40 SCRAPER OPERATION**

AT THE GENERAL MOTORS TRAINING CENTER
PATTERSON, CALIFORNIA · DATE Dec. 18, 1964

IN

SERVICE TRAINING SUPERVISOR · SERVICE TRAINING REPRESENTATIVE

In November 1960, Clem was elected business manager. To address one key safety issue in 1961—proper training—Local 3, state and federal agencies, and local schools began to step up their apprenticeship program. The program called for three years of training on the job supplemented by "related classroom instruction." It was approved by Local 3, the AGC, the Engineers and Grading Contractors Association, and the state of California in October. The first class of engineers-to-be began. This class was soon followed by many more and would eventually lead to the building of the Rancho Murieta Training Center (RMTC).

By May of 1963, Local 3's safety program was so successful it received the National Safety Award from the IUOE. This award "recognizes leadership, initiative, and originality in promoting accident prevention on a year round basis by newspapers, magazines, radio and TV stations, and outdoor ad agencies." The *Engineers News* was cited as a key component for the success of the program.

In 1964, automation, designed to free workers from repetitive tasks, was actually stealing food from union members' mouths. Two million jobs had been lost to "labor-saving" devices—the automated hand controlled by the computer

◀ *Certification for TTSS-40 Scraper Operation for William H. Genn, Jr. (Courtesy of William H. Genn, Jr.)*

brain. Congress, recognizing that something needed to be done to stave off a recession, created the National Committee on Technology, Automation, and Economic Progress to study the effects of automation on the economy. Despite the misconception during the Korean War that Manpower acts were "manpower grabs in times of war," this time they provided much needed funds for Local 3.

Based on the findings of the committee, the Department of Labor released nearly $250,000 of the funds, authorized by the Manpower Development and Training Act, to provide training in "blade operations, rubber-tired equipment, catskinning, heavy repair work, and grade-leveling." This funding would eventually allow Local 3 to launch a unique pilot program designed to upgrade the skills of its members.

Nearly 300 members from Local 3 and Local 12 completed six-week courses at Camp Roberts near Paso Robles. Apprenticeship training and skills-upgrade programs were increasingly important to provide the best construction hands in the industry.

However, they didn't get the money without a fight. Recognizing that additional government money could be had, the National Association of

▲ *Clarence Cleaver (front row, far left) in a training class at the local community college in the 1960s. (Courtesy of Clarence Cleaver)* **Top Right** ▶ *Camp Roberts mechanics in training. (Courtesy of Al Dalton)* **Bottom Right** ▶ *Camp Roberts Graduation in 1966. (Courtesy of Charles Odell)*

UNITED STATES DEPARTMENT OF THE INTERIOR
BUREAU OF RECLAMATION

TRINITY DAM DIVISION - CENTRAL VALLEY PROJECT

TYPE	EARTH FILL	VOLUME OF MATERIAL IN DAM	33,180,000 CUBIC YARDS
STRUCTURAL HEIGHT	537 FEET	ELEVATION OF CREST OF DAM	2,395
HEIGHT ABOVE STREAMBED	465 FEET	ELEVATION OF CREST OF SPILLWAY	2,370
CREST LENGTH	2,450 FEET	RESERVOIR AREA AT MAXIMUM NORMAL STORAGE	16,400 ACRES
MAXIMUM WIDTH AT BASE	2,962 FEET	MAXIMUM RESERVOIR CAPACITY	2,500,000 ACRE FEET
WIDTH AT CREST	40 FEET	USABLE RESERVOIR CAPACITY	2,160,000 ACRE FEET
DRAINAGE AREA	688 SQUARE MILES		

6,000,000 TRUCK MILES WILL BE TRAVELED TO PLACE ALL THE MATERIAL IN THE DAM

IT WOULD TAKE 815,000 TRAINS OF 100 TANK CARS EACH TO HAUL ENOUGH WATER TO FILL TRINITY RESERVOIR. THE REQUIRED TANK CARS WOULD REACH AROUND THE WORLD 26 TIMES.

THE DAM WILL BE AS HIGH AS A 40 STORY BUILDING AND 2 EMPIRE STATE BUILDINGS LAYED END TO END IN THE RIVER CHANNEL WOULD BE COMPLETELY COVERED IN THE DAM.

Home Builders (NAHB) tried to convince President Lyndon B. Johnson that an independent training program should be created. The unions, it claimed, had failed to produce skilled craftsmen. Clem went to bat for Local 3, countering that NAHB's intention was to set up "substandard construction trades programs" with taxpayer money, and that the union would produce craftsmen "as soon as the jobs are created." The battle between the unions and big business over how government money should be used for training would be fought again and again in subsequent decades.

In 1965, Local 3 had its "worst safety record in history." Thirty-two industrial accidents had resulted in deaths. Realizing that many of these deaths could have been prevented by basic first aid training, Local 3 embarked on a first aid training program. In one year, this program became the " . . . largest in the nation's history, where a labor union and the Red Cross have teamed up to help stamp out unnecessary deaths caused by ignorance of good First Aid and safety methods." Once again, Local 3 rose above and beyond the challenge.

Opposite Page ◀ *Work on the Trinity Dam in 1960. (Courtesy of Betty Rhodes, wife of John Rhodes, who worked on the dam for the 1959 and 1960 seasons.)*
Left and Right ▲ *First aid classes at Camp Roberts.*

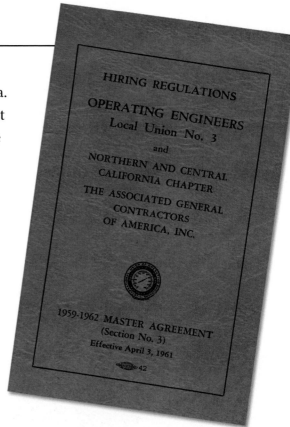

In February 1964, the Local 3 Credit Union was chartered by the state of California. It offered union members a low-cost way to borrow money by charging an interest rate of no more than 1 percent per month. This benefit was later extended to include Nevada, Utah, and Hawaii. The credit union allowed members to buy necessities and luxuries without worry, as is evidenced by letters written to the *Engineers News,* including this quote from member George T. Hardwick: "I financed my trailer with the Credit Union and was well-satisfied."

At about the same time, the Local 3 Pension Plan had grown to 708 happy retirees. In August 1965, Congress enacted Social Security health insurance designed to help younger people still at work as well as retired and widowed families (Medicare). Interestingly, this act passed despite the objections of the American Medical Association (AMA). In the '50s, the AMA came out against increased disability payments and now opposed Medicare.

Issue of Safety

The first Safety Award was for "100,000 Safe Man" hours and was given to the members who worked on the 19th Avenue Freeway job.

Safety "When the tool's not right, the guy's not bright." Governor Edmund G. "Pat" Brown Sr. named June 1961 Apprenticeship Month, thereby launching a program …"to improve the quality of apprenticeship...!" The motto for Apprenticeship Month was "For Tomorrow's Skills – Train Today. "

In 1963 Local 3 was picked for U.C. Research Study for its outstanding safety project. "Build a better mousetrap and they'll beat a path to your door."

By January 1967, the pension plan raised payments to a maximum of $200 per month or $8 a month for each year of pension credits, leading one pensioner, Lew Peck from Fallon, Nevada, to write: "… after forty-six years in construction it is very nice now that I'm retired to enjoy things a person dreams about." In 1969, Local 3 signed a "Reciprocity Agreement" with the company administering the pension plan. This agreement allowed members to carry over pension credits earned while working outside Local 3's jurisdiction, with another affiliated local in 13 western states. More money for some!

Opposite Page ▶ *Surveyors break for a group shot on what was to become the Rancho Murieta Training Center in the later 1960s.*

"*Those who would destroy or further limit the rights of organized labor — those who cripple collective bargaining or prevent organization of the unorganized — do a disservice to the cause of democracy.*"

John F. Kennedy

▲ *Driving pile for subway line under Oakland's Lake Merritt.*

Bay Area Rapid Transit (BART), a space-age, high-speed monorail that nowadays snakes beneath the surfaces of San Francisco, Oakland, and Berkeley, zooms alongside cars stuck in gridlock and shoots under the Bay, was arguably the largest dredging and construction challenge Local 3 faced in the 1960s.

Construction officially began in 1964 with a test section between Walnut Creek and Concord dedicated by President Johnson. For two years, engineers tested the high-speed tracks and computer programs used to run the system. Finally, in 1966, work began on the most crucial component of the system, the Transbay Tube. For months, artist renderings of the tube posted in the *Engineers News* mystified members—how would this impossible mission be accomplished? In April 1967, the dredging began.

The men on the trench job were hand-picked deep-water magicians. They were dredger men who would "have their hands full, fighting choppy water, wind, and changing tides while trying to control a free-swinging bucket on a 100-foot boom . . . they can't see what they're digging; they just do it by feel." The clamshell dredge they used was affectionately known as "Thelma."

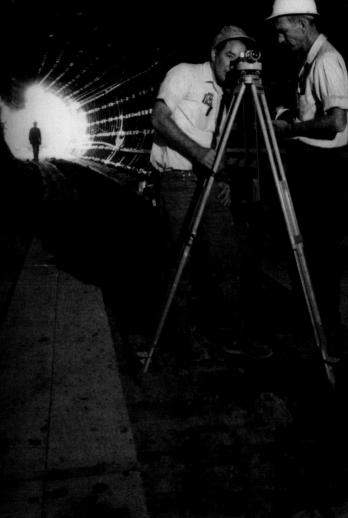

Above Top Left ▲ *Tunnel entrance at the Stanford linear accelerator.* **Above Top Right** ▲ *Building the roadway girder for BART. (Courtesy of Cronk & Associates)* **Bottom Left** ▲ *BART tracks under construction.* **Bottom Right** ▲ *Putting new tracks in place for BART system.* **Right** ▶ *Surveyors in the Berkeley BART tunnel near the Hayward earthquake fault.*

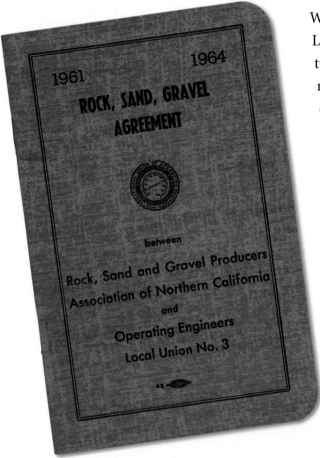

Work on BART was stalled from time to time by political shenanigans; however, Local 3 kept busy on several preparatory projects, including the 3.1-mile twin tunnels through the Berkeley Hills. This project was expected to be one of the most hazardous of the BART projects, but Local 3 completed it one month ahead of schedule with no loss of life. BART trains began running officially in mid-1972. True to form, the city of Berkeley stayed faithful to its environmental and political roots by opposing some of the initial planning for construction in the city.

Many of the projects Local 3 worked on during the 1960s were the direct result of the cold war. In the spring of 1961, three titan missile bases were completed near Marysville. The silos for these giant missile launchers were 120 feet deep from the open cut and 45 feet in diameter with 16 underground supporting structures to house personnel, fuel equipment, and tracking antenna, all connected by a labyrinth of tunnel 60 feet under ground.

Another cold war project began in October 1961 in Palo Alto. Local 3 began work on the Stanford "Atom Smasher" project, approved by the Atomic Energy Commission and estimated to cost $114 million. The Smasher (Nuclear Accelerator) was installed underground at a 400-acre site in the Stanford Foothills. Upon its completion in 1967 the *Engineers News* described the accelerator as the "longest pea shooter in the world."

The need for water projects—both the containment of water and the movement of water—continued to be a high priority for California and the nation. When completed, the Oroville Dam, described as the "key unit of the nation's first statewide water project," would be the highest "embarkment" dam in the world and highest dam of any kind in the United States.

Opposite Page ▶ *Two 50-ton Clyde Whirly cranes pour concrete at the Thermalito Powerhouse, part of the huge Oroville Dam, which was completed in 1968.*

▲ *All Photos including Opposite Page* ▶
Apprentices work and learn at the Rancho Murieta Training Center.

Pension Trust Fund
of
Northern California, Northern Nevada, Utah,
Hawaii, Guam and the Mid-Pacific Islands
of Operating Engineers
Local Union Number Three
of the International Union
of Operating Engineers, A F L - C I O
cordially invites you to attend
Dedication Ceremonies
of Rancho Murietta Training Center
on Saturday, November fifteenth
Nineteen hundred and sixty-nine
at eleven o'clock in the morning
Sloughhouse, California

Entertainment
Refreshments, Western-style
Barbecue

R. S. V. P.
415/431-9843

The necessity for these water control projects was heartbreakingly underscored in 1965 when a devastating flood hit the Eureka area. Brothers Ray Cooper and Curly Spence wrote: "Cities along Highway 101 have completely disappeared; bridges have collapsed under pounding debris floating in the raging flood waters of the Eel, Mad, Klamath and Trinity rivers; livestock have given up to torrential waters and are washed up with bloated bodies into silted deltas created over highways that are no more . . . as if some giant clamshells from the sky gulped chunks out of them." In California, politicians were slow to learn the lessons that both the 1955 and the 1965 floods should have taught them. They would continue to drag their feet on funding projects necessary to prevent the death and destruction caused by flooding.

Throughout most of the 1960s, Local 3 seemed content to steer clear of the raging anti-war and civil rights battles. But they were in tune with the need to provide equal opportunities for all. In 1967, they created a pre-appenticeship program, which was designed ". . . to provide pre-apprenticeship training for one-hundred and twelve culturally disadvantaged youths from hardcore employment areas of Alameda."

All Photos Opposite Page ◀ *Construction at the Rancho Murieta Training Center.* Left ◀ *Invite to the dedication ceremonies of the Rancho Murieta Training Center, November 15, 1969. Below* ▼ *Scraping and leveling the site at the Rancho Murieta Training Center.*

Politically, Local 3 maintained a low-key presence, primarily because a Democratic, pro-union president and governor ensured a period of union growth and relative stability. However, in 1966, Local 3 was uncharacteristically silent as union favorite Governor Edmund "Pat" Brown was defeated by Ronald Reagan. Just four years earlier, Local 3 issued a strong endorsement for Brown against his Republican challenger, Richard Nixon: "For four straight years," wrote Clem, "California has balanced budgets without any new taxes in the last three of those years—and in fact, with some tax deductions." Local 3's silence during the '66 elections may have been due to Clem's support for Reagan, a man who shared his views on the threats of affirmative action and the "ecology" movement; a man he thought would lower taxes and "get the chiselers off the relief rolls."

In the Pacific Islands, Guam began to get some notice around Local 3 as they struggled to organize the island. In 1966, the governor of Guam, Manual F. L. Guerrero, rose to national prominence by vetoing Right-to-Work legislation. The veto was supported by President Johnson who said "the bill would inhibit development of the free collective bargaining necessary to protect and advance the welfare of working men and women of Guam."

◀ *An old Mission in Guam, where membership reached 800 in February 1968.*

As the 1960s came to an end, reports from members working on various construction projects in Vietnam began to trickle into the *Engineers News*. Ross Mossholder: "This is a war of patience where U.S. and Viet Cong mix red blood in an earth of red gumbo. It is far from being a new war as all wars are hellish." Another unnamed member wrote ". . . jungles are hot and full of leeches, red ants and termites that bite people instead of wood."

In 1968, Nixon, a man who previously couldn't be "elected dog-catcher," won the republican nomination for president. Nixon campaigned as the "New Nixon," a pro-working man and anti-tax crusader; however, members were warned not to be misled by the "poor loser who engages in tirades against the press." Indeed they were right. After he won the election, Nixon's empathy for the common man seemed to quickly fade away.

Also in 1968, the state legislature passed and Reagan signed the Myers-Milias-Brown Act (MMBA), governing labor relations in local governments allowing public employees a voice in their wages, hours, pension, holidays, and all other terms and conditions of employment with their employer. This meant Local 3 and other unions could represent, bargain, and fight for the rights of the public sector workers. This began the Public Employee division of Local 3 that continues to this day with more than 8,000 public employees. One of the first law enforcement groups to be organized by Local 3 was the Santa Cruz County Deputies, which joined in 1971.

By October 1969, the true impact of Nixon's presidency on unionism and the economy hit union officials smack dab in the gut. As a part of the Tax Reform Act of 1969, Nixon proposed a devastating 75 percent cutback on construction projects. The resulting boost in unemployment, he smugly announced, was necessary to curb inflation. The unions were outraged that he had so little empathy for the human and social problems of unemployment.

They deplored the fact that he intended to keep wages steady and freeze highway projects, putting working class families in jeopardy while he blithely ignored rising steel and copper prices and bank rates that had soared from 6.5 to 8.5 percent. "If they can put a man on the moon, how come they can't figure how to control inflation without throwing people out of work?" became the question of the day. Despite the great stride and growth made in the 1960s, without highway and construction projects, Local 3 faced a grim future.

"Survival Under Atomic Attack"

In a sign of the times, on the front page of the January 1951 issue of the *Engineers News* an ad for a bomb booklet titled, "Survival Under Atomic Attack" can be found stating that every family member should read this booklet so that all of the people will be prepared if attack comes. As the US prepared for a possible third world war in the early 1950s, the defense industry employers were negotiating for a 12-19 cent raise while they were issuing "dog tags" costing 26 cents with the name, address, blood type and religion.

However, the '60s were a decade of continued growth for Local 3, and despite the prospects of losing highway construction projects, the decade ended on a look to the future, training future operating engineers. Years of planning and hard work throughout the decade culminated in the completion of the RMTC at Sloughhouse, California, 20 miles southeast of downtown Sacramento, which was ready to house and train 48 apprentices.

Opposite Page ◄ *Operators in front of the Local 3 OJT Contractor Hall. (Courtesy of Charles Odell) Above* ▲ *Senate commendation to Business Manager Al Clem for his outstanding efforts in labor leadership, August 8, 1968.*

Additions To The *Engineers News* In The 1960s

- **Get acquainted Feature** – with biographies of different union officers.
- **Consumer Advice** – what to buy, how to avoid getting ripped off.
- **Engineers at Leisure** – spotlight on hobbies of members (most were into cars).
- **Apprentice Corner** – updates on the Apprentice Program, sometimes Star Apprentices honored.
- **The Swap Shop** – free advertisements for members.
- **On the Safety Side** – Dale Marr, discussing on-going need to exercise caution and report any abuses. Updates in safety procedures.

Above ▲ *Gold Dredger Number 21 was photographed in 1968 on the final day of its operation on a dredge pond in Yuba County. The dredge was the last of a line built by Wendell P. Hammon, a local farmer who decided to get into the gold mining business at the turn of the century. Local 3 members who operated No. 21 and the rest of the fleet dredged over one billion cubic yards of material during the 68 years of the company's operation, yielding over $137 million in gold. Opposite Page* ▶ *The Bucyrus-Erie Wheel Excavator at the San Luis Dam at Los Banos, California, from May 1964 to November 1967. It ran 24 hours a day on three shifts. It was the largest machine ever used on a construction job up to that point in time. (Photo courtesy of Curtis Brown. He operated the excavator on the swing shift.)*

Bucyrus-Erie Wheel Excavator Specifications

Total Weight – 815 tons
Maximum Height – 64 feet
Wheel Diameter – 30 feet
Wheel Speed – 2 to 8 r.p.m.
Buckets on Wheel – 10 each 2 1/2 c.y.
Belt Widths – 84 inches
Tracks – 6 feet wide by 29 feet long
Horse Power on Travel – 750 h.p.
Horse Power on Wheel – 750 h.p.
Horse Power Each Belt – 300 h.p.
Digging Conveyor Length – 43 feet
Stacking Conveyor Length – 63 feet

Hailed as "another progressive step in the total training concept envisioned by Union No. 3 and the employers by whom its members are employed," this facility was built on 3,500 acres purchased by the Operating Engineers Pension Trust Fund. The money for the daily operation of the center would come from the Affirmative Action Trust Fund offices in San Francisco; however, day-to-day operations would be handled by the Joint Apprenticeship Committee (JAC). This

Left Top and Bottom ◀ *The Bucyrus-Erie Wheel Excavator at the San Luis Dam at Los Banos, California. (Photos courtesy of Curtis Brown. He operated the excavator on the swing shift.)*

committee was a cooperative effort of Local 3, the AGC of Northern California, the Engineers Grading Contractors Association, and the Bay Counties Engineer and Land Surveying Association.

▲ *John Rhodes working on a project on Highway 299. (Courtesy of Betty Rhodes)*

As reported in the *Engineers News,* "Not since the bloody forays of bandit chieftain Joaquin Murieta whose name still rings out on these rolling hills and the swish-swish of a thousand gold pans in the Consumes River had this small community witnessed such a big event." On November 15, 1969, 1,400 people attended the dedication of the new facility, watching as a team of skydivers, led by Operating Engineers Paul Schissler and Pete Kalthoff, members of the amazing Golden State Skydiving Team, entertained them. This team had 3,050 collective jumps in competition with the nation's best skydiving teams. They gave an exhilarating exhibition of their skills as they slowly and methodically fell to earth. Dignitaries such as Mayor Joseph Alioto of San Francisco, Mayor Richard Marriot of Sacramento, IUOE President Hunter Wharton, and of course Clem spoke at the event. Clem was introduced to the assembled dignitaries as "a man concerned not merely with the heroic role of unionism in hours of adversity, he is a man who recognizes that unionism also has the responsibility of acknowledging industrial change."

As Local 3 celebrated its 30th anniversary, the future looked uncertain, with both inflation and unemployment on the rise; however, through a decade of steady growth, the union gained the trust and respect of its members, and together they knew they could survive whatever came their way.

The Operating Engineers would face new challenges in the 1970s—challenges it didn't expect or even see coming, challenges that would pit the union against some of the very people whose lives it had worked hard to protect. Operating engineers were rightfully proud of their contributions to society: water control projects that not only provided energy but also helped prevent floods and provided water during droughts; highway projects that eased congestion and allowed people to get to and from work safely each day.

But social movements that began in the 1960s—the environmental, equal rights, and women's liberation movements—were growing from infancy into rebellious, idealistic movements of the new generation. This became evident particularly in northern California where men working on highway and water control projects heard screams and angry words from these energized groups for "wanting to pave over the world." Jobs were lost as legal shenanigans halted or shut down projects completely. It would be a frustrating and difficult decade for Local 3. But it would also be an enlightening decade as more minorities and women began to make their way into training programs and eventually onto jobsites. Local 3 would become a leader in creating opportunities for a diversified membership unlike any in the IUOE.

The decade began with the same policies from Washington DC. Inflation was on the rise and, as had happened in previous decades, there was talk of a wage freeze for federally funded programs. The Nixon administration also called on the states to "voluntarily freeze" new highway projects. On behalf of Local 3, Business Manager Al Clem traveled to Washington DC. He and other union leaders, such as AFL-CIO President George Meany, informed President Nixon that freezing wages would be paramount to "rubbing more fat into the hides of those who are already too fat." In 1971, despite the pleas from union leaders, Nixon imposed a wage price freeze on federally funded programs and asked governors for voluntary freezes on state highway projects.

Opposite Page ◀ *Ronald Reagan and Business Manager Al Clem in April 1973 at the dedication of the Rancho Murieta community development built with the help of the Rancho Murieta Training Center. Above* ▲ *Ralph Lakes on the job.*

Knowing that a freeze on highway projects would mean difficult times for Local 3, Clem urged members to take advantage of the apprenticeship programs at the RMTC in between jobs. He even arranged for the credit union to provide low-interest loans for members who needed help paying the $6-a-day room-and-board expenses for the six-week training course. "This is no Mickey Mouse operation," he promised, "but affords the finest site, most modern equipment, and top experts in both classroom and equipment instruction to be found in the country."

RMTC continued to grow and gain notoriety through the 1970s. In addition to the Rancho Murieta mobile home village, opened in December 1972, plans were underway for a 4,000-foot air strip; eight recreation-oriented lakes and reservoirs; a 160-acre equestrian center/rodeo arena; bridle, bicycle, and foot paths; a Huck Finn Island Playground; beach areas along the river; and historical sites on the RMTC property.

As the decade progressed, environmentalist and no-growth fanatics began halting more and more highway and water control projects. Finally, Local 3 decided to fight back. They picketed the home of a Contra Costa County congressman who had proposed an amendment that would shut down water control projects on the Trinity and Eel rivers in northern California, projects that had been approved after devastating floods of the '50s and '60s. Clem accused the congressman of blatant hypocrisy as without such water control projects, his own Contra Costa District "would still be salt marshes, and he would have to pass an amendment giving the Killdeers the vote." It was not a matter of "jobs versus the ecology" he complained, when these projects would prevent flooding, saving lives and millions of dollars of property damage. But the damage had already been done.

In 1972, there was a glimmer of good news for Local 3. Plans were underway for the construction of a rock fill dam called the New Melones Dam on the lower Stanislaus River. This project would bring long-term jobs to Local 3 at a time when many highway jobs were on hold and a new "Coastal Initiation" threatened to

RECIPE - 1971
SAN FRANCISCO COLE SLAW

SHRED ONE HEAD OF CABBAGE INTO A LARGE BOWL. ADD TWO SHREDDED CARROTS TO THAT. ADD ONE SHREDDED APPLE TO THAT. ADD TWO TABLESPOONS SESAME SEEDS, OR 1/4 CUP CHOPPED WALNUTS TO THAT. LIGHTLY SALT AND PEPPER. MIX IN ABOUT TWO TABLESPOONS MAYONNAISE. ADD ENOUGH APPLE CIDER VINEGAR TO MAKE THE SALAD TO YOUR TASTE. MIX, COVER BOWL, REFRIGERATE UNTIL READY TO USE. FOR A MORE TART SALAD, ADD A LITTLE DICED ONION AND GREEN PEPPER. FOR A SWEETER SALAD, ADD SOME RAISINS

▲ *Recipes were a common feature in the Local 3 calendars during the late 1960s and early 1970s.*

Above All Photos ▲ *Work at the New Melones Dam on the lower Stanislaus River. (Courtesy of Bob Beall)*

"*The most important thing for the local to survive is leadership, organizing and integrity. Those qualities should spread across the entire organization – from the officers to the apprentices.*"

Ken Green, member

94

impose a five-year moratorium on "virtually all construction within a thousand yards of any body of water subject to tidal action." The New Melones Dam project had the full support of the California Fish and Wildlife Department. The lower Stanislaus River was in danger of dying due to overpopulation in the area. However, companies running white-water rafting tours on the lower Stanislaus opposed the dam. Together they joined a group called Friends of the River to try to stop construction based on ecological concerns. Their motive had more to do with "dollars in their eyes" than saving the river.

In an attempt to work with the environmentalists to head off further conflicts, Clem met with the Sierra Club. They agreed to participate in a study group with Local 3 to try to see if they could find middle ground; however, this did not prevent the Sierra Club from going ahead with plans to block several projects, including the Devil's Slide bypass.

Clem was facing reelection that year, and with the economy and job situation souring, tensions were high. He had been business manager since 1960 and, despite questionable health, decided to run for reelection. One of his challengers was Norris Casey, a former business agent, district representative, and one-time conductor out of Oakland and Nevada. In the regularly scheduled election of 1972, it appeared Casey would win, as he led the election by about 300 votes with only the Hawaii and Guam votes yet to be counted. But something smelled rotten. Even before the ink had dried on the Hawaii votes, Casey contested the ballots before they were counted. These challenged ballots gave Clem 1,434 votes to 201 for Casey, with Clem winning overall by 900 votes.

Opposite Page ◀ *Work at the New Melones Dam on the lower Stanislaus River. (Courtesy of Bob Beall)* *Above* ▲ *Rally in support of the Highway 101 bypass in South San Jose.*

TWENTY-NINTH CONVENTION
OF THE
INTERNATIONAL UNION
OF
OPERATING ENGINEERS

It took nearly nine months from when the election was contested to get a ruling. The similarity in ink and in signatures on many envelopes containing individual votes, in addition to the way the votes were counted and other irregularities, was enough to overturn the election in mid-1973 as unlawful. A new election was scheduled for November of that same year, this time under the watchful eye of the Department of Labor. As a result, Clem decided not to run for reelection, throwing his weight and support to Assistant Business Manager Dale Marr for business manager. As the nominations were readied for the rerun election, the other candidates for business manager were Martin Casey, Norris Casey, and Paul Edgecombe. Norris Casey lost to Marr by a slim margin of 122 votes. Clem retired on November 30, 1973.

Dale Marr
Business Manager 1973 – 1982

In April 1973, despite the uncertainty in the air as a union election was about to be overturned, Governor Ronald Reagan made a grand and glorious visit to RMTC, delivering a speech filled with amusing anecdotes to reaffirm his commitment to unions. At that time, Reagan had a strong relationship with Local 3, even announcing at the annual AFL-CIO meeting held that year in San Francisco that he was ". . . clearly in the camp of the working man" and against the "anti-progress extremists."

Norris Casey,
challenger in contested election
in 1972

In October, the first Old Timers' Day at RMTC drew a crowd of 647 members and their wives for a tour and lunch—roast beef, mashed potatoes, and peas. This event soon became an annual event, now called the Retiree Picnic. The menu is still the same.

▲ *Business Manager Dale Marr and California Governor Jerry Brown at the Lakeside Club at the top of the Kaiser building in Oakland, California.*

The 1970s saw the increased use of Local 3's print shop on Valencia Street in San Francisco by local political candidates. The two-color Heidelberg press was used to print union forms, bylaws, and other union-related materials to support the membership and increasingly for the printing of literature for candidates and propositions.

Soon after winning the repeat election, Marr, who'd been responsible for Local 3's successful safety program, vowed to reorganize the union and put the politics of the recent election behind him. The changes he put into place were designed to create more effective business agents, stewards, and health and welfare administrators. "We're clearly past the time when we can call a man off the seat of a piece of equipment, give him a set of keys and some credit cards, and tell him he's an agent," he explained. Almost immediately he assigned a representative full time to the "momentous" task of figuring out the newly revamped but still complex Occupational Safety and Health Administration (OSHA) regulations.

Another reform of 1974 was the inclusion of a cost-of-living clause in negotiated contracts. In May, Local 3 decided to weigh the pros and cons and have a vote. On the plus side, the

Left ◀ *Ronald Reagan and Business Manager Al Clem at the dedication of the Rancho Murieta community development built with the help of the Rancho Murieta Training Center. Above ▲ Hank Morikawa shakes hands with the president pro tempore of the California State Senate, David Roberti, in the Local 3 print shop on Valencia Street, San Francisco, California.*

clause would provide for a wage boost when the national consumer price index increased beyond a certain number of points over a given time period; however, there was a slim chance the index would decrease. Not surprisingly, members voted "overwhelmingly in favor" for the Cost-of-Living Clause.

The gubernatorial elections of 1974 provided a different kind of challenge for Local 3. In the primaries, Local 3 endorsed Mayor Joseph Alioto of San Francisco, a long-time friend of labor. But he was beaten by Edmund G. (Jerry) Brown, a man who openly supported Proposition 17, a scheme backed from the river rafting companies to halt the long and eagerly awaited New Melones Dam project.

Despite their reservations, after meeting with Brown and receiving assurances he would create a government agency to mediate between environmentalist and other concerns, the Local 3 leadership took a deep breath and publicly endorsed him for governor.

Happily for Local 3, Proposition 17 was defeated, and Brown was elected as "the youngest governor in California history." His relationship with Local 3 during his next four years as governor would be, to say the least, rocky. The tension began early the next year (1975) when Local 3 accused Brown's new transportation chief of "being at war against people and their automobiles." She had "blue-lined" several highway projects from the budget, projects that Local 3 was counting on in a bad market.

The Nuclear Power Initiative was another issue on which Local 3 accused Brown of taking a pro-environmentalist stance. This initiative would have prohibited the construction of new nuclear power plants and phase out the operation of existing ones. Local 3 argued that in light of the current energy shortage it would probably be defeated, but not before delaying many projects, perhaps for months. "The effect of a nuclear plant ban," Marr argued, "would be felt by nearly every household in the state." The initiative was defeated but not before several projects had been held up.

> ### Words of wisdom from Jerry Brown's father, Governor Edmund G. "Pat" Brown Sr.
>
> "First, you feed people who would go hungry without your help. Second, you put those people back on their feet and third, you start wiping out the conditions that broke their spirits and their homes in the first place."

Meanwhile, the state legislature was considering the passage of the Farm Labor Bill of 1975, which would provide farm workers the same rights to organize as other unions. This bill caused many a shouting match between the AFL-CIO, the Teamsters, and the United Farm Workers (UFW). At issue was a missing "true craft protection clause" that would protect non-UFW workers, including Local 3 members who worked for firms that did as high as 90 to 100 percent of their work in agribusiness fields. Due to the mediating efforts of Brown, the bill was later modified and signed.

Although Brown's mediation of the Farm Labor Bill would help win him Local 3's endorsement in the 1978 elections, it was not the end of conflicts between him and the union. Projects, such as the San Felipe Dam and Dumbarton Bridge, were still being delayed by environmental issues, with Brown accused of "sitting on the fence." However, many large highway projects, including I-580, were beginning to get the green light. Things were looking up for Local 3.

In 1976, as the hope for new jobs increased, Brown was again accused of being anti-union. His California Job Opportunity Act, designed to help minorities break into the construction industry, was strongly opposed by

Top Left ◄ *Dedication ceremony in 1972 of the Foresthill Bridge that crosses over the American River.* *Bottom Left* ◄ *Rancho Murieta Training Center class in the early 1970s.*

Marr. He accused Brown of trying to "put non-union workmen, most of who would not have been trained, on public works projects." In doing so, Brown was "using the frustrated aspirations of ethnic minorities and women with the implied promises of jobs." Further adding insult to injury, the Brown administration was considering providing a taxpayer-funded apprenticeship training program, an action that drew this statement from Marr: "It is unfair to expect our journeymen to pay in taxes for a state apprenticeship program when they are already paying for a first-rate apprenticeship program in their own union."

Despite these shenanigans, there was room for compromise that put more people to work, even if they were working on an art project. The Christo "Running Fence" project was one such project. Some thought it a work of genius, a 24-mile, 18-foot-tall wall of white nylon fabric that billowed in the breeze for two short weeks before being dismantled. Others thought it was, well in a word, Nuts! The project lasted 42 months from the planning stages to the completion of the fence. Construction began on April 29, 1976, and the Operating Engineers who worked on Christo's Running Fence built across 59 ranches in Marin County, would never forget the experience. Local 3 member Harold Puckeylow worked on the project during the planning and construction phases and was responsible for the radio communications. He said, "It was the most unusual job I had ever worked on in my life. It was a lot faster tearing the fence down than building it from scratch. Some of the local people thought it was crazy, but it was an exciting project. Christo donated all of the materials to the ranchers, and if they didn't want it, he had it hauled away when the fence was torn down."

During the last few years of the 1970s, new Environmental Protection Agency (EPA) standards designed to clean the air and water brought both a curse and a blessing to Local 3. Many of the projects Operating Engineers hoped to work on were delayed, because the projects did not meet federal EPA guidelines. The largest of these projects was the Dow Chemical expansion project, which would have brought hundreds of jobs to Bay Area engineers. In

Opposite Page ◀ *Field Day at Tenco Tractor at Pleasant Grove, California on June 13, 1975. It was the first CAT D9H that the dealer received. Tenco was organized in April 1965. Back row, from left: Richard Bartlett, Samuel Horsley, Teddy Wherry, Geo. Nichols, Jr., Richard Mordido, and Don Ewards. Front row, from left: Quallie Jones, Larry Estrada, Doug Warnock, and Stephen Douglas. (Courtesy of Teddy Wherry) Above ▲ Christo and Jeanne-Claude's running fence in Marin County in September 1976.*

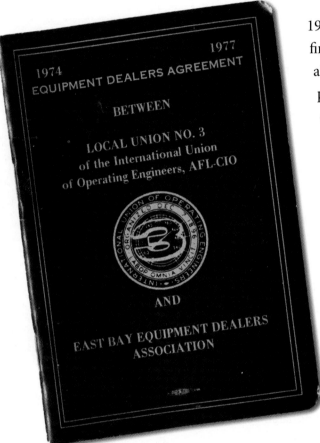

1977, Dow Chemical finally tired of fighting the EPA and pulled out of the project. At first this was a big blow to Local 3; however, many existing sewage treatment facilities also did not pass EPA standards and would need to be upgraded. These upgrade projects meant more jobs for Local 3, jobs that would not be picketed or stopped by environmentalists. For once, Local 3 and the environmentalists were on the same side.

By early 1977, California was beginning to suffer from the effects of a two-year drought. The drought was so severe that water officials in Marin County began to encourage neighbors to spy on each other and report violations of the county's strict water-rationing rules. The drought had a silver lining for Local 3. Many environmentalists who had helped defeat bonds that would have put more water in Warm Springs Dam and spared Marin County a lot of misery became realists about the need for water control projects. At long last, the job situation for Local 3 was about to turn around. That spring, the California Department of Transportation (Caltrans) began to "free up" even more highway, canal, and water control projects, including highways 4, 580, and 680 in the Bay Area.

After years of skirmishes between labor and environmentalists, it was Congressman Leo Ryan from the San Francisco Bay Area who finally came up with a solution. In 1977, he proposed that the Operating Engineers be put to work on dam safety programs for which there was a "crying need." Unfortunately, he died trying to save people from the Jonestown cult before many of his proposed programs could be put into place. In the words of Marr, his death was "a great loss to the labor movement . . . a true friend to Local 3, and he came to our aid on many issues that were important to our members."

Opposite Page Inset Left ▶ *Scrapers removing the mountain of dirt to be used in the building of the dam. Opposite Page Inset Middle ▶ Approximately 35 double engine push/pulls worked on the Warm Springs Dam. Opposite Page Inset Right ▶ The hopper at Warm Springs Dam. Opposite Page Background Photo ▶ The day shift, swing shift, and office crew of the Warm Springs Dam Project 1978-1982. There were 180 belly dumps and 35 scrapers running full bore on the dam. Dirt was brought down by conveyor belt to place in dam. (Courtesy of David A. Harlan)*

WARM SPRINGS DAM
PROJECT
1978 — 1982

▲ *Members and their families strike against Builders Concrete, Inc.*

In February 1978, as work was set to begin on the Warm Springs flood control, environmentalist groups again waged "guerilla warfare" against Local 3, filing lawsuits guaranteed to "tangle a proposed project indefinitely." As these legal battles raged in court, the Russian River went on a rampage. Floodwater peaked at 39 feet, forcing residents of Guerneville from their homes and causing millions of dollars in property damage. Enough was enough. Many congressmen and justices were beginning to see what these lawsuits were actually costing the taxpayer. In March, with the help of Congressman Dan Clausen, the project was able to resume again.

In the spring of 1978, despite "strong objections," Local 3 decided to support Governor Brown in his reelection bid. For four years the relationship between the union and the Brown administration had been up and down. Governor Brown was a man whose strong environment philosophy they felt had "driven countless businesses and thousands of jobs from the state;" however, he had been willing to sit down and negotiate some difficult compromises, including the Farm Labor Bill.

In October 1978, the issue facing Local 3 members in Battle Mountain, Nevada, was not because of the environmentalists but because of a pressing need for higher wages and a cost-of-living increase. A four-month strike was reaching a fevered pitch, especially

after the strikers' demands were met with a 3 percent raise, a 25-cent cost-of-living increase, and a reduction in benefits for those employees over 65. Rocks were thrown and a few Local 3 members were arrested, found guilty, and fired. The union had to file charges with the NLRB in order to get the situation resolved.

The following month, Operating Engineers in the Bay Area began work on the new Dumbarton Bridge project, a project that was touted by Marr to be "... one in a string of projects." The old Dumbarton Bridge was a 50-year-old structure, straddling the low water at the south end of the San Francisco Bay. The new bridge would consist of 75-foot pre-stressed concrete spans hauled up from Visalia, California, and built 90 feet north of the old one. The project would include improvements to nearby approaches and streets.

That same month, just before Thanksgiving, San Francisco was rocked by the tragic murders of Mayor George Moscone and Supervisor Harvey Milk. Mayor Moscone had supported Local 3 on many projects, including the huge Yerba Buena project in downtown San Francisco that was set to start the next year. Part of this project was a $100

Above Left ▲ *Grizzly Forebay Tunnel.* *Above Right* ▲ *A diamond bit mole used in digging a tunnel. (Photos courtesy of David Harlan)*

"*You have to remember that Hawaii was only a territory up until statehood was achieved in 1959. No governmental agency gave any priority to a "territory"…they couldn't even vote. We had to push the NLRB to even hold an election.*"

Harold Lewis, former officer

million, state-of-the-art convention center that would revitalize the area south of Market. The convention center was renamed Moscone Convention Center in honor of George Moscone, "a true friend to labor."

The decade ended fittingly with Local 3 members pulling together to raise more than $150,000 for the City of Hope's Occupational Health Program. City of Hope began as a non-sectarian pilot medical center. It was founded in 1913 by trade unionists on the basic concept that "medicine is a human right." Today, the City of Hope is a world-class biomedical research and treatment institution located in the foothills of the San Gabriel Mountains near Los Angeles. For his part in the fundraising effort, Marr was presented with the "Spirit of Life" award.

In the 1970s, Local 3 fought many battles just to be allowed to work on projects for the public good. Nature helped them with droughts and floods that illustrated the benefit of their work. But the so-called "champions of the environment," who had begun their fight in the '60s, entered the '70s with blinders on. They were obsessed with returning to a time of untouched wildernesses and pure mountain streams, dreams which all men share, but, Operating Engineers lived in the real world. They knew there was no going back, only forward with a spirit of hope that they could conquer all challenges, known and unknown.

Opposite Page ◀ *Moving a pipe into place in Hawaii in 1979. Above Left* ▲ *View of the bridge construction over the New Melones Reservoir. Above Right* ▲ *Completed construction of the bridge across the New Melones Reservoir. Bridge construction continued despite the controversy over construction of the New Melones Dam in the late 1970s. (Photos courtesy of Bob Beall)*

By 1980, Local 3 was ready for a changing of the guard, from the many years of union policies under Al Clem and Dale Marr to the progressive policies of Tom "T. J." Stapleton. It was also a time of excess and growth, both personally and professionally for Local 3 and its members. The person responsible for many of Local 3's changes in the '80s was Stapleton, who was elected business manager and officially sworn in on September 1, 1982. Previously the union's recording-corresponding secretary, Stapleton ran on the Green Ticket, to defeat former Vice President Bob Mayfield by a 52 to 48 percent margin.

Changes started happening very early in the 1980s. In January 1981, Local 3 again took the forefront in innovative programs by announcing the establishment of a new Alcoholic Recovery Program (ARP) to help members who needed assistance or counseling to help with an alcohol abuse problem. This program later became the Assistance and Recovery Program and included help with substance abuse. The program, one of the first of its kind among unions in the United States, was a voluntary program that provided referrals to various treatment programs.

Drug and alcohol abuse was not a new phenomenon to society at large but, in the era of "Just Say No," Nancy Reagan's project in support of the war on drugs, it was increasingly on the minds of members and employers. The *Engineers News* regularly printed information about different substances and what they did to a person's body and mind. By the end of the decade, the controversial subject of drug testing was proposed to mixed opinions. Some members thought it smacked of communism; others thought it was long past due. General tips to stay healthy also started to appear in later editions of the *Engineers News*. Ways to cut fat from one's diet, quick exercises, and preventative health care were discussed. An article in the April 1988 issue of the newspaper was titled "Go for your goal: Quit smoking."

Opposite Page ◄ *A TV camera crew interviews a Local 3 member about the rock, sand and gravel strike in Fresno, California, in 1982.* ▲ *Bob Mayfield (middle) services the members while coming out of a mine.*

Staying healthy encompassed preventing injuries on the job as well. For example, in 1982, members were regularly warned about modern-day hazards, such as working under power lines, and among buried high-voltage electric lines and natural gas lines.

Local 3 was also at the forefront in hazardous waste training. While hazardous materials had been present for years, it wasn't until 1986 that Congress passed legislation to protect workers engaged in hazardous waste operations. The law included specific provisions for initial and routine training of employees before they engaged in an operation that could expose them to safety and health hazards, but Local 3 took the lead in providing training to union representatives in hazardous waste. In February 1988, Safety Director Jack Short and Business Agent Tom Hester attended an 80-hour course at the Mine Academy in Beckley, West Virginia. Immediately following the course, Local 3 put together the first 40-hour training course in Redding. Thirty employees of local contractors, most of them Local 3 members, attended an eight-hour-day, five-day training program that certified them for hazardous waste operations.

The program focused on ways of identifying toxic substances and the protection needed to work safely and correctly around various kinds of wastes. This class, as well as an expanded Hazmat program, continues today.

Because safety was at the forefront of the '80s, it was quite a surprise when, on July 1, 1987, California's Governor George Deukmejian pulled the plug on the state's Occupational Safety and Health Administration (Cal-OSHA). Immediately, Local 3 backed the campaign to restore the program "100 percent." In fact, according to newspaper articles at the time, no labor-led campaign drew more support from such a diverse cross-section of California society as the fight to restore Cal-OSHA.

Top ▲ *Business Manager Tom Stapleton addresses the members following his swearing-in ceremonies in 1982.*
Bottom ▲ *Assembly Speaker Willie Brown reviews the contents of the special briefing on infrastructure with Local 12 Business Manager Bill Waggoner, left, and Local 3 Business Manager Tom Stapleton, right, in 1983.*

Just a year after its demise, the effects of the closure were already evident. The state's Senate Committee on Industrial Relations revealed that deaths among private-sector workers increased 53 percent in the first six months after Cal-OSHA was dismantled and its responsibilities handed over to federal OSHA. Work-related deaths in the public sector, which remained under the jurisdiction of the scaled-back Cal-OSHA, decreased 40 percent in the same six months. Funding for the program was reinstated in May 1989.

Cal-OSHA's first big job following reinstatement occurred not too long after—on November 28, 1989, a crane collapsed in downtown San Francisco, killing four operators and a bus driver and injuring 21 others. A Pecco "lufting" tower crane located at a high-rise project on 600 California Street in the heart of the city's financial district suddenly began to swing out of control as ironworkers were in the process of "jumping" the crane, or when the tower lifts the operator—cab, jib, and all—up into the air so a new tower section can be slid underneath and bolted into place.

Left ▲ *An operator works on a 37-mile aqueduct in Utah in 1982.* *Right* ▲ *Tunnel workers monitor the concrete as it is pumped into the form for a seven-mile-long tunnel as part of the 37-mile aqueduct in Utah.*

Realizing something was wrong, crewmembers yelled to the operator to stop the boom's swing, but to no avail. The crane's 160-foot boom swung away from the building and slammed into an office high rise across the street. The collision ripped the boom housing and counterweight from the crane's vertical support and pulled huge steel girders from the high rise and chunks of concrete from two neighboring buildings as the structure plunged 16 stories to the streets below. Four construction workers fell to their deaths. A school bus driver was crushed when the crane's housing landed on the bus she was driving. In light of this disaster, Local 3 pushed for more intense crane certification, resulting in legislation that required a license for any crane operator before operating any equipment.

All this safety training couldn't prepare the union for the hazards ahead in the political arena. Politics in the 1980s were tough on labor. President Ronald Reagan's landslide defeat of presidential incumbent Jimmy Carter in 1980 signaled an attack that left the trade union movement decimated throughout the country. Slowly but surely, basic worker protections and the legal rights of unions eroded.

Left and Above ▲ *Construction and rescue crews clear away fallen debris in an attempt to reach crew members who fell to their deaths in the tragic crane collapse in San Francisco, California in 1989. Opposite Page Inset* ▶ *The "Betty L", a 420' long heavy lift derrick and pipe-laying barge on it's maiden voyage to Ocean Beach in San Francisco in late February 1983. (Courtesy of Vernon Baumbach) Opposite Page Background Photo* ▶ *Less than two weeks after beginning its work at Ocean Beach on the Southwest Ocean Outfall Project for the city and county of San Francisco "Betty L" was struck by an unexpected strong storm on March 3, 1983. A full crew, including several Operating Engineers, were working on board. Fortunately, although there were some serious injuries there were no fatalities. It took eleven months of shipyard repair before the "Betty L" went back to work. (Courtesy of Vernon Baumbach)*

During the Reagan administration, the labor picture was bleak. Republican influences on federal judges created a powerful conservative alignment that blanketed all aspects of federal labor law. Labor decisions coming out of the courts and the NLRB were very anti-union.

In response, unions stopped relying on the NLRB and the courts as they had in the past and put more effort in the traditional and proven weapons of labor—the strike, the picket line, and the boycott. Political strategy became all important with labor unions, as a proven way to fight right-wing politics is to elect union supporters into office. Unfortunately the struggle would not end with Reagan. In 1989, his vice president, George H. W. Bush, would succeed his boss as president and serve through 1993, continuing many of Reagan's policies and opposing labor's fight for justice. But labor wasn't always on the losing end.

In 1987, following the most intensive lobbying effort Washington DC had seen in years, the unions won a huge battle. Not one but both houses of Congress voted to override Reagan's veto of an $87.5 billion highway finance bill, a bill the president labeled "pork-barrel politics at its worst." Reagan had primarily objected to the $890 million for 121 local projects, including mass transit and road jobs, jobs badly needed by operating engineers.

Left ▲ *Operating Engineers working on the 3,000-acre Skywalker Ranch in Lucas Valley, California in 1980 for "Star Wars" creator George Lucas. This Local 3 crew was perhaps the most photographed bunch in the 1980s, as nearly every week, Lucas' crew filmed the project's progress. A stationary camera on one of the hillsides even took time-lapse photographs of the project. *Right* ▲ Members take a well-deserved break on one of the dirt spreads for the Redwood Bypass job through the Eureka area in 1987.*

Members' Opinions Regarding Mandatory Drug Testing
(Engineers News **February 1988)**

"Drug abuse is so great now that drug tests should be made without question. The drug testing should be done twice to insure that a mistake is not made causing the employee problems that are not warranted."

"No Drug Testing! We are not a commie country yet. We do have rights."

"If drug testing is needed to ensure safe working conditions, do it!"

Representatives of the building trade unions, the construction industry, the AGC, state highway commissions, and transit officials swept Washington in an effort to obtain the support of Republican lawmakers who were crucial to any override attempt. After a presidential veto, two-thirds of both houses of Congress must agree to an override in order for a bill to become law.

Mission accomplished. Many projects were completed because of the override. In California, projects included the $35 million John Knox Freeway between I-80 and the Richmond/San Rafael Bridge, and the $30 million renovation of a stretch of Highway 99 north of Sacramento. Northern Nevada received $51 million for highway projects. Utah received more than $107 million in 1987 and $750 million over the five-year life of the bill. Included in this was money for two jobs on the east-west Belt Route in Salt Lake City for $40 million, I-70 north-south in Richfield for $5 million, and $30 million for resurfacing and bridge reconstruction statewide.

In 1986, Caltrans led its largest single highway project to date: the Redwood National Park Bypass project, located about 40 miles outside of Eureka. This project was a job operators didn't soon forget, as it presented many challenges. Working on rugged terrain with many steep grades, thousands of huge redwood stumps were uprooted, cleared, and burned with tons of small growth that also covered the project site. The ground was extremely unstable at many places, as the soil retained a high moisture content, making compaction difficult to contain. The weather also made things tough for workers with foggy, wet, and cold days. And this was usually in the summer! The long, wet winters on the North Coast placed even more severe restrictions on the work season.

▲ *Comic about the executive salaries in 1988, as published in* Engineers News.

"When I first went to work in the union, there was a war against organized labor in the Reagan administration. That shaped us into survival mode. We shrunk a little but survived."

Bill Burns, former officer

In 1988, Local 3 worked on a project of a completely different type, this one also in the redwoods. Work on the Prison of the Redwoods, now called Pelican Bay State Prison, broke ground in early 1987. Three contractors spent almost $30 million just to clear 240 acres of second-growth trees and stumps left behind by previous logging, install utility lines, build internal roads, and erect a warehouse on the Malarkey Forest site.

Meanwhile in Hawaii, many large-scale projects were underway. Road construction in Hawaii, which would have been virtually shut down if the highway bill hadn't passed, included work on the Wailoa River Bridge project in Hilo valued at $17 million. In January 1987, Hawaiian members broke ground on one of their biggest projects ever, "Ko olina," a $2 billion, 1,015-acre West Beach resort that included an 18-hole golf course, 5,200 homes, 8 hotels, a marina, and 18 acres for commercial use. Its name meant "fulfillment of joy." To get this project started, many Local 3 members worked hard, sacrificing their own time attending hearings. They would have their joy when the project was complete!

Another large-scale, first-of-a-kind project for Hawaii was the H-Power garbage-to-energy plant. The brainchild of Hawaiian Dredging, the $195 million power plant was expected to turn waste into energy and produce electricity cleaner than oil-fired plants at the Campbell Industrial Park. The plant was the most expensive public works project in Honolulu's history at the time.

Opposite Page ◀ *Operators perform early work on the Redwood Bypass project in the Eureka area, the largest single highway project ever let by the California Department of Transportation in 1986. Above Left* ▲ *An operator moves mud in San Mateo, California in 1983. Top Right* ▶ *Equipment breaks up the earth as part of a housing development project. Middle Right* ▶ *A Local 3 backhoe operator cuts a trench during construction of a new sports arena for the Kings basketball team in Sacramento. Bottom Right* ▶ *An operator performs trench work on a storage pond in Santa Rosa, California in 1983.*

Hawaii members were also busy on a highly controversial project: the H-1 freeway. After more than 30 years and more than $506 million, the H-1 interchange freeway was completed in 1986. H-1 enabled Oahu motorists to travel about 27 miles from Kahala to Palailai. The freeway also connected Pearl Harbor, Hickam Air Force Base, and Barber's Point Naval Air Station.

As seemed to happen at least once in every decade, northern California experienced one of its worst floods in the winter of 1986. This flood would put hundreds of Local 3 members to work, repairing levees and riverbanks throughout the state, rebuilding major parts of Highway 70 in the Yuba City area and repairing the damage of homes and, in some cases, entire communities. The storm began on February 13, 1986, and pounded northern California relentlessly for a week. There had been other storms, like the one in 1982 that crippled Marin and Santa Cruz counties, but the 1986 storm was the "granddaddy," dumping so much water in just one week that the state's rivers, streams, and reservoirs swelled far beyond their limits.

Levees on the Sacramento, American, and Feather rivers built to hold flows of thousands of cubic feet per second, received more than they were designed to withstand. In Sonoma County's Guerneville, the Russian River reached an unprecedented 54 feet, giving the resort community the worst dousing in its history. The Napa River also overflowed, and the Sacramento Delta took a beating. Tyler Island, Dead Horse Island, Rio Linda, and North Sacramento were a few of the areas flooded out. Highway 70 in the Feather River Canyon was torn to shreds—more than

Right ▶ *Local 3 members pick up the pieces in San Rafael, California in 1982 after a huge storm hit the San Francisco Bay Area.* *Opposite Page* ▶ *A Hawaiian dredging crew works on the Westin Kauai Resort project in Hawaii in 1986.*

"Air conditioned cabs were a novelty. On the floors of some of the equipment, the temperature would be 242 degrees. You had to have gloves to get out."

Jerry Bennett, former officer

One of the largest continuous concrete pours in the history of Utah construction in 1981.

18 miles of highway had to be rebuilt from scratch. The flood devastated the counties of Santa Cruz, Sonoma, Mendocino, Humboldt, and Del Norte, as well as the Central Valley and the San Joaquin Valley. Flooding was so severe in the community of Linda that some sections of town remained 6 feet underwater a week after the levee broke.

Santa Cruz was hit the hardest of all. At least 22 people were killed by the storm, most buried in the gigantic mudslides in the Love Creek and Ben Lomond areas. More than 400 people were displaced, 135 homes demolished, 300 others seriously damaged, and at least 50 businesses were either damaged or destroyed.

Local 3 members were once again called to help clean up the destruction and put the area back together. Work crews seemed to be everywhere in Marin County. Just four days after the storm, the company had more than 50 loaders, dozers, backhoes, scrapers, and blades working in emergency cleanup operations throughout the county. The storm's damage in Marin County was second only to Santa Cruz in its intensity.

California suffered more damage when the Loma Prieta earthquake rocked the San Francisco Bay Area on October 17, 1989. The quake caused severe damage, most notably in San Francisco and Oakland, but also in Alameda, San Mateo, Santa Clara, San Benito, Santa Cruz, and Monterey counties. A reported 18,306 homes and 2,575 businesses were damaged. According to reports, the quake caused an estimated $6 billion in property damage, becoming one of the most expensive natural disasters in U.S. history at the time.

Local 3 once again provided much of the work to restore and repair the area. In fact, a project agreement was worked out between Local 3 and a Texas contractor that assured that union workers would perform the first phase of earthquake repair work on the Cypress portion of the Nimitz Freeway.

Local 3 members were on the front lines almost immediately, conducting dangerous rescue efforts on the collapsed Nimitz Freeway. They made emergency repairs to ruptured water and sewer lines and demolished unsafe buildings. Members ran critical security operations and braved the elements to begin repairs on the Bay Bridge. Within hours of the earthquake, crane operators were at the Nimitz Freeway to begin shoring up collapsed sections to make it safer for rescue workers. Once again, the union donated money, giving $50,000 to the American Red Cross to assist victims of the earthquake and set up an earthquake relief fund to channel additional aid to worthy charities providing assistance to quake victims.

Although the mid-1980s seemed full of disasters, there were some projects that gave Local 3 construction rather than cleanup work. After more than six years of legal and environmental wrangling, the San Francisco Redevelopment Agency finally received the go-ahead to oversee the $1 billion Yerba Buena Gardens urban renewal project. This marked the first time in the city's history that a labor-management project agreement had been negotiated for a major, privately funded project. The historic pact covered the three phases of the Yerba Buena Center, a project that stretched over six years. At the time, Yerba Buena Gardens was one of the largest projects in San Francisco's history.

Top ▲ *Operating Engineers make repairs to the Lake Elman Dam in the Santa Cruz Mountains following the October 1989 Loma Prieta earthquake.* *Bottom* ▲ *The Office of Emergency Services (OES) Cypress Command Post included many Local 3 public employees in 1989. These members helped with the rescue and repair of the San Francisco Bay Area after the Loma Prieta earthquake shook California.* *Right* ▶ *Two cranes work on the 22-story Circus Circus Tower project in Reno, Nevada in 1981.*

Construction workers were honored for finishing the second unit of the Hunter Power Plant in about 1982 – ahead of schedule and accident free. The plant was located just a few miles outside of Castledale, Utah. David Hardman was part of the OE3 Technical Engineeer Team under Dick Houston, one of several brillant OE3 Technical Engineers. (Courtesy of David Hardman)

The project took up 24 acres of downtown San Francisco property between Market and Folsom and Third and Fourth streets. In return, it was expected to generate $19 million in new taxes and more than 2,000 construction jobs.

A California project in the '80s that meant a lot of work for Local 3 members was the North Fork Stanislaus River Hydroelectric Project. Tucked away in the high sierras, the job provided work for more than 120 Operating Engineers. Stretching over about 40 miles of the North Fork of the Stanislaus and related tributaries, the $268 million project began in the spring of 1985. Work included a diversion dam immediately downstream from the confluence of Silver and Duck creeks, a diversion tunnel leading to Spicer Meadows Reservoir, and the Spicer Meadow Dam, located on Highland Creek with related diversion tunnels and a powerhouse among others.

In September 1986, for the first time in a long time, the Sacramento District had several big highway jobs going on at the same time. Operators were working on the Highway 65 bypass through Roseville and on Highway 99, which was undergoing a major expansion to four lanes just north of town.

The $57 million Highway 65 project called for the construction of a new interchange on I-80, a 1.4-mile section of the four-lane freeway and 2.5 miles of four-lane expressway. Operators moved about half-a-million yards of material, mainly river rock and sandstone. The much-needed bypass had been on the drawing board for more than 30 years. The California Transportation Commission finally approved it in 1980 to relieve severe traffic congestion through downtown Roseville. The bypass created about 30,000 new jobs and allowed for 44,000 new homes over the next two decades. The bypass was dubbed the Harold T. "Bizz" Johnson Expressway, in honor of the retired congressman who represented the citizens of Roseville and was instrumental in obtaining the necessary funding for the project.

I-80 just past the Highway 65 bypass became a major project one year later with a $27.6 million, 2.1-mile widening project that broke ground in Auburn in the fall of 1987. The previous four-lane freeway, originally built in 1947, was a bottleneck for a number of years. The widening project was a welcomed relief for traffic while completing a gap in the upgrading and widening of the major trans-Sierra freeway.

▲ *A gradechecker works on a major Highway 99 expansion project in Sacramento, California in 1986.*

Local 3 members in the Bay Area also kept busy with major highway projects. The state's biggest construction program was in Eureka, however. California highway officials reported in the *Engineers News* that the $1 billion, six-year, statewide highway expansion effort would also include $2.7 billion to help deal with the explosion of traffic in the Bay Area. Ironically, although from 1980 to 1986, the number of registered vehicles in San Francisco jumped 20 percent, Caltrans had only spent $694 million on highways in the Bay Area.

Also during this six-year period, work included a $30 million, three-year project to add a lane on both sides of the Benicia Bridge; a $241 million project that included adding a new carpool lane between Ashby Avenue in Berkeley and the Bay Bridge; a $493 million project to extend Highway 85 from Stevens Creek Boulevard in Cupertino southeast to I-880 north of Los Gatos, and east to link with Highway 87 and Highway 101 in southern San Jose; and a $250 million project to transform Highway 237 from a stop-light-studded road into a six-lane freeway with interchanges.

It was a busy time for Nevada members too, as four major reconstruction and overlay jobs on eastern Nevada highways began at the end of 1986. Covering close to 41 miles, more than 70 operators stayed busy on $13.5 million worth of road work. The longest job was by Las Vegas Paving Company on I-80 at Emigrant Pass and covered 11.82 miles. Further to the east on I-80, G-P Construction had a 3.5-mile overlay job at the Pequop Summit that cost just under $2.5 million. Frehner Construction of Las Vegas had a $2.35 million overlay job on Alternative Highway 50 south of Wendover at the Nevada/Utah state line that extended more than 14 miles. G-P Construction had an 11.5-mile, $2.5 million job that included moving close to 150,000 yards of dirt outside Carlin.

As construction grew, so did the inside workings of the union—most significantly at this time was the introduction of computers and electronics. While the public's access to the World Wide Web and e-mail would come later, internal programs began "going electronic." In 1983, the Fringe Benefits Center celebrated a big first when they began a new "online" program consisting of two computers!

The Foundation for Fair Contracting (FFC) was another product of the 1980s. Spearheaded in 1984, the job-monitoring program was established to monitor California's underground economy in the construction industry. By 1986, it had developed into an extremely effective weapon to combat abuses against workers and was still used in that capacity in the 21st century.

Stapleton explained the program: "Many employers who have received fines and stop-payment notices because of information that the Foundation helped to obtain are under the mistaken impression that we are merely out to harass non-union firms. This is not true. The Foundation for Fair Contracting is a joint-effort by the union and signatory employers to see that the law is enforced and that the underground economy in the construction industry is eventually eliminated."

▲ *Construction workers turned out on April 17, 1985 at the Reno City Hall in downtown Reno in support of repealing the bill to abolish Nevada's Prevailing Wage Law. (Courtesy of Ed Jones)*

In the mid-1980s, Local 3's efforts to enforce Davis-Bacon prevailing wage laws in Utah were commonly met with delays and red tape. Being a business agent was a hazardous job at times, but this story gives that concept a whole new meaning. The job became life-threatening in 1986 with the attempted murder of Local 3 Business Agent Jasper Delray. Twice.

The first attack occurred in September 1986. Delray was investigating complaints he received about prevailing wages not being paid on a Forest Service road improvement project in a remote canyon in Sanpete County. Delray discussed the case with employees on the project and, on his way down the canyon road, "all of a sudden something hit my windshield," he recounted in the November 1986 edition of the *Engineers News*.

"At first I thought it was just a rock that had flipped up and hit my car," he said. "When I realized that someone was shooting a gun at me, I hit the brakes, opened the door and rolled out of the car and laid down in the ditch next to the car."

Four shots hit his vehicle before he could escape—two hit the windshield, one hit the quarter panel behind the left-front wheel, and the fourth shot hit the driver's door about waist-high. According to the paper, this shot would have hit Delray had it not been deflected by the door brace. Delray stayed in the ditch for about 10 minutes before he felt safe enough to get to a phone and call the police. Two slugs were eventually retrieved from Delray's vehicle and turned over to the sheriff's department for evidence.

A second incident was reported that November. Delray was targeted again, this time while leaving the home of an employee who worked on the Forest Service job. He was visiting the operator to take a statement on prevailing-wage violations. On his way out of town, he was tailgated by two vehicles and eventually run off the road and into a 25-foot ravine. He told the *Engineers News* that the driver of one of the two vehicles involved was pointing a gun at him.

On a more positive note, Utah staff and members had no problem at all going to work on the long-awaited Jordanelle Dam, which broke ground in the summer of 1987 after 25 years of planning. Part of the Central Utah Project, the dam was located six miles north of Heber City on the Provo River and was built to store 320,000 acre-feet of water to be used in Salt Lake City and northern Utah counties. The dam provided work for about 1,200 people during its peak years from 1989 to 1990.

Overall, the 1980s were a time of excess, both in the workplace and out. Plenty of projects kept our members busy as infrastructure and roadwork became priorities, but being busy did not prevent problems with drugs and alcohol. A changing of the guards was necessary to help move Local 3 into the position to deal with these problems. But Washington engaged in excess as well, and the unions also paid for it, as the erosion of their power began and continued throughout the decade.

That "excess" behavior was prevalent outside of work as well, as drug and alcohol abuse was on the rise nationwide. Local 3 was ready to combat it by introducing new drug and alcohol abuse programs and drug testing on the jobsite. It was definitely a time of change, but as the country adapted, the union forged ahead.

Right ▶ *An operator steps out of her loader for a moment on the I-215 Beltway project in the Salt Lake Valley in Utah in 1988.* *Opposite Page* ▶ *Working on a Hyatt Regency Hotel in San Francisco. (Courtesy of Joe Wendt)*

Even with all the tension and strife unions faced, American workers can look back at the '90s as a decade of prosperity born of strong economic growth and low unemployment. It was a decade when huge advances in technology, specifically the miniaturization of computers, helped bring the future into focus. It was a decade that ended with advancements in cell phone and Internet communications, which would help boost grassroots organizing and political campaigns. And finally, it was a decade when natural disasters, such as the Oakland Hills firestorm, El Niño, and the Loma Prieta earthquake, and manmade disasters, such as the crane accident of 1989, would lead to a huge demand for stricter rules and regulations.

Training and safety preparedness were once again top priorities in all areas from dirt jobsites to hazardous waste cleanup. On the heels of the tower crane collapse in San Francisco that killed four construction workers and injured 21 others, Business Manager Tom Stapleton began the '90s with a strong push toward passing a crane-licensing bill. At that time, inspections on crane safety were done by private agencies, usually those employed by the owners and manufacturers of the equipment they tested. Testing had to be done by an outside inspector under government oversight; otherwise more tragedies would occur.

Cal-OSHA, the agency in charge of enforcing occupational safety standards, was in the hot seat in the early '90s; closed in 1987 because of "disengagement" by Governor George Deukmejian, it was later reinstated in May 1989. After a thorough investigation, Cal-OSHA cited the crane company for 25 alleged violations regarding the horrific accident.

In the '90s, Local 3 had to stay politically sharp to avoid suffering from the effects of former President Ronald Reagan's free-enterprise philosophy. This philosophy was hurting the labor economy at home by sending more and more manufacturing and service jobs abroad. Things were just as bad for unions when his successor, President George H. W. Bush, began using the same anti-labor tactics, bringing about a huge increase in the wage gap between corporate giants and the working class.

Opposite Page ◀ *Members move tons of dirt for the Gale Ranch Project in Dougherty Valley, California in 1997.* ▲ *A member casts his vote about the dues proposal in 1990.*

In California, politics of a different kind were coming to a close with the addition of Unit 12 state workers to the IUOE and Local 3. After a long search for representation with a number of unions throughout the '80s and into the '90s, California's state bargaining unit known as "Unit 12" chose representation from the IUOE, which in turn is an affiliated union of the AFL-CIO. State Unit 12, a collective bargaining unit of all of the crafts, maintenance, and allied job classifications of employees within the state civil service system, was looking for good representation.

According to Garth L. Magnum and John Walsh in *Union Resilience in Troubled Times*, the onset of major public employee representation from the IUOE was the consequence of a Supreme Court's decision in 1991 claiming that "skilled maintenance employees" were viewed as bargaining units. The result was "10,500 California state employees all in one state-determined bargaining unit, Unit 12, and all dispersed throughout the state in blue-collar occupations." These units had been represented by a number of unions during the '80s, including the California State Employees Association (CSEA). However, because of their diverse job classifications among other things, in a statewide vote, Unit 12 members voted to determine that the IUOE and their affiliation with the AFL-CIO were able to provide the best representation possible for this diverse group of employees across the state. As a result, IUOE Locals 3, 12, 39, and 501 were approved to represent Unit 12 in their respective regions in California.

Opposite Page ◀ *Highway 40 paving crew in 1990. Left* ◀ *Unit 12 bridge tow truck operators keep drivers safe in 1995. Above* ▲ *A crane operator pauses in 1990 for a candid photo.*

"*You would drink 2½ gallons of water a day, but lose it all because of the heat. If you were over 35, you couldn't run a scraper. You had to be young and crazy. They would open the throttle and run it into the ground.*"

Jerry Bennett, former officer

In 1992, after receiving massive support from Local 3, democratic nominee Bill Clinton was elected president, marking a possible return to good times for the union. Clinton promised to be more sympathetic to workers' problems and to provide more government regulation to protect workers, tax relief for middle-class families, and more spending for public works and infrastructure.

Clinton honored his word by proposing a short-term economic stimulus package in 1993. He also signed an order banning striking worker replacements, which gave strikers peace of mind to further their cause without fear of being permanently replaced. However, his good intentions were thwarted when in 1996 an appeals court consisting of judges appointed by Bush and Reagan nullified this order.

Despite political setbacks, the union continued to organize and act on behalf of their own. As a result, in April 1993, 40 Turlock canal workers won a blistering $2.4 million judgment over proper payment of overtime against their employer, and in August of the following year, after successful negotiations, the second-largest construction company in Mendocino County signed a contract with Local 3.

All in all, the '90s were a busy time for Local 3 members with plenty of work to be had. They found themselves hard at work on projects ranging from highway improvements and housing developments to airports, ballparks, and even the 2002 Olympic Park in Utah. Highway projects included several I-5 related jobs and interchanges worth $115 million that brought the highway up to interstate standards from the Mexican border to the Canadian border.

Another highway project worth mentioning was the work done on Highway 101. The job entailed increasing a stretch of road between Willits and Ukiah known as the Cloverdale Bypass from two to four lanes and meant working on dangerous cliffside slopes in a vertical canyon. The job called for catskinners, men who operate equipment with caterpillar treads or a bulldozer. Although the job was dangerous, for the catskinners there is no such word as "can't." They are a breed of hearty souls, dating back to the early days before Local 3 was born.

In the early '90s, despite a recession caused by Reaganomics and a soft housing market, open farmland rapidly gave away to large, expensive subdivisions, such as Laguna West in Elk Grove, the Rancho Palomares Subdivision between Castro Valley and Hayward, and the hard-fought-for Kealakekua Ranch Project in Honolulu. The home building surge east of Sacramento (along Highway 50) was also indicative of how housing and commercial construction were picking up elsewhere in northern California.

Top ▲ *A lubeman finds the problem on a jobsite in 1990. Bottom* ▲ *Shop mechanics in the San Joaquin Valley in 1994. Right* ▶ *President Bill Clinton stands with a Local 3 family in 1996.*

Local 3 would also be involved in efforts to renovate Devil's Slide, a stretch of highway in San Mateo County that is geologically unstable. As its name implies, many lives have been lost as mud loosened by heavy rains poured over the road, sweeping cars over the cliff to the rocks below. Stabilization projects had been on and off since the 1970s, blocked primarily by groups such as the Sierra Club voicing environmental concerns. Eventually, in the late '70s, Devil's Slide received the go-ahead and some improvements were made. However, to this day, Devil's Slide remains a long-standing source of employment for Operating Engineers.

▲ *Labor cartoons were often featured in the* Engineers News. *Right* ▶ *A 1990s dragline in action.*

137

Airport renovation also kept Local 3 members busy from California to Utah to the Keohole Airport in Hawaii. One of the biggest airport jobs was the renovation of the San Francisco Airport, which employed more than 2,300 construction workers—craftsmen who had to be precise as the billion-dollar project was crammed into an area the size of a shopping mall.

One of the larger road-widening jobs in 1990 required 300,000 yards of excavation on Highway 152 in Santa Clara County.

During this decade, the Bay Area was indeed the site of a disproportionate number of large-scale projects and improvements. Money was streamlined to the Bay Area to the tune of $2.4 billion for upgrade work nearly every year, making it, at the time, the heaviest construction concentration in the United States. One of the most notable additions was the San Francisco Giants' ballpark, Pac Bell Park, an icon in a city famous for history, bridges, and parks.

Projects also boomed in Utah and Nevada. Utah was in a flurry of planning for the 2002 Salt Lake City Olympics. This was the second time in the century that members of Local 3 had worked on an Olympic project; the first being the 1960 Squaw Valley Olympics near Truckee, California. The 2002 Salt Lake City Olympics project was a massive undertaking that took nearly seven years of preparation, which included building the event's 120-meter ski jump, the luge and bobsled tracks along with miles of trenches for the snow-making tracks. To move more than 1.6 million spectators, athletes,

▲ Members work on the Oroville Airport runway in California in 1994. (Photos courtesy of Teddy Wherry)

officials, and journalists fluidly throughout the region, the Utah Department of Transportation (UDOT) received between $900 million and $1 billion in federal aid for Olympic transportation. In Nevada, the Tuscarora Pipeline, another big-name project, employed 250 Operating Engineers. Their job was to build the pipeline from northeastern Nevada to the Reno-Sparks area.

Every decade has its share of disasters, both manmade and natural, and the '90s were no exception. Local 3 saw conflict abroad during the Gulf War and in politics at home, as well as earthquakes, hurricanes, floods, and firestorms. As in previous decades, natural disasters always resulted in an all-out relief effort from the Operating Engineers. Local 3's finest rose to the task of aiding fire-ravaged neighborhoods, seismic-retrofitting a bridge, or renovating older structures after earthquakes.

▲ A blade operator smiles for a photo on the job for Calaveras Pipeline in 1993.

Repairing the damage from these disasters creates hundreds of jobs and points out the need to alter the design and completion of current projects. For example, after the Loma Prieta earthquake in 1989, San Francisco's Embarcadero was labeled unsafe. The city's mayor at the time, Art Agnos, spearheaded its demolition and replaced it with a six-lane subsurface expressway.

Local 3 has always been a supporter of our military efforts overseas and the Persian Gulf War was no exception. Initially known as Operation Desert Shield, it eventually led to Operation Desert Storm. Its intention was to prevent an invasion into Saudi Arabia. This war from August 1990 to February 1991 had a profound effect on the lives of some Operating Engineers. After Iraq's occupation and annexation of Kuwait, a coalition force from 34 nations led by the United States expelled Iraqi forces from Kuwait. Members David T. Stevens and Dave DeWilde were featured in the *Engineers News* after they returned. Stevens returned as part of Desert Shield and DeWilde returned from Saudi Arabia with the 940th air refueling group. Operation Desert Storm became one of the largest military mobilizations since the Vietnam War.

On October 20, 1991, the 1,800-acre firestorm in the Berkeley-Oakland hills felt like a war of its own. Local 3 employers removed hundreds of burned-out vehicles, scorched trees, and power poles. Through the week of October 27 through November 2, members worked from 7 a.m. to dusk, plucking an average of 25 vehicles a day from the rubble of destroyed homes.

Hawaii had its own share of natural disasters; most fearsome were the "strong and piercing winds" of Hurricane Iniki, which ravaged Kauai on September 11, 1992. This Category 4 hurricane damaged or destroyed thousands of homes, cut off power for weeks, injured or killed a dozen people, and destroyed at least one resort. Local 3 contributed $50,000 to the Red Cross to aid its members.

A disaster of a different sort happened on a soggy evening in March 1995. The Arroyo Pasajero Bridge on I-5 near Coalinga collapsed as water raged through a normally dry creek and washed away the underpinning of the twin bridges, killing seven people and cutting a major thoroughfare between northern and southern California. Caltrans had a dilemma on its

▲ *Caltrans contends with a tanker truck explosion on Cypress Street in San Francisco, California in 1995. (Photo courtesy of the* San Francisco Chronicle*)*
Opposite Page ▶ *A Delayed Gas Hydro Treater (DGHT) fractionization column is lifted at a Shell Refinery in 1995.*

hands: how to build a temporary bridge over a sandy and unstable culvert. The solution was to use railroad flatcars. This was not a new idea as there are 83 such bridges in California, some of which date back to the 1930s. These bridges are typically located on low-volume, local roadways. This temporary bridge allowed the freeway to stay open while Local 3 members were able to build a new bridge in 33 days—17 days ahead of schedule.

Two years later on New Year's Eve 1997, the National Weather Service station in Monterey, California, warned of a major storm brewing 1,500 miles out in the Pacific. The storm hit with such ferocity that it caused water to pour over the Don Pedro Dam Spillway for the first time in 26 years. California highway systems suffered nearly $300 million in flood-related losses that sent union contractors straight to work.

These floods were caused by a weather phenomenon known by a popular buzzword of the time "El Niño." It kept Operating Engineers busy, with the state spending millions of dollars in repairs of roads, rehab of flood control, and El Niño-proof renovations.

In state politics, California Governor Pete Wilson stirred up a firestorm of his own in 1995 when he made the mistake of trying to abolish prevailing wages. He began attacking federal, state, and local statutes that require contractors on public works projects to pay their trades people—union or non-union—wages and "prevailing" wages in the area where the project is located. Prevailing wages are frequently at or near union scale and make it possible for a union employer to bid competitively on public works contracts. In protest, 15,000 people, including 2,000 Operating Engineers, marched to the steps of the state capitol to give Governor Wilson a message: hands off prevailing wages!

Later in the decade, Wilson would also be responsible for introducing the infamous Proposition 226. This proposition threatened to slow down labor's ability to gain projects and would in effect rig the bidding system to help the state—

Opposite Page ◄ *More than 15,000 labor activists march at the California state capitol in 1996 on Valentine's Day to tell Governor Wilson to keep his hands off prevailing wages.* ▲ *Members rally in support of prevailing wages at the California state capitol in 1996.*

not the union—gain engineering and architectural contracts. Once again, Local 3's political mobility paid off and Proposition 226 was thwarted. It should come as no surprise that in the 1998 gubernatorial elections, Local 3 came out swinging in support of democratic candidate Gray Davis.

On the national level, by the end of the 1990s, union membership had fallen from a high of one-third of all employed people in 1945 to 13.9 percent. This factor, as well as Local 3's increasing contributions to political campaigns, caused financial losses, which could lead to cuts in services for members. In an effort to increase union membership and thereby alleviate the problem, Organizer Bob Miller launched the first Construction Organizing Membership Education Training (COMET), a political mobility grassroots organization designed to regain bargaining and political strength.

Poor and spotty media coverage was identified as one reason for the decrease in union membership. And so, Local 3, with the support of the IUOE, began creating grassroots media campaigns, such as filming a promotional video for the IUOE. They also created a list of media contacts the membership could call with news or when/if they saw biased, inaccurate reporting about unions.

▶ *The "iron" lines up for another subdivision during the nation's late 1990s housing boom.*

"Everyone wants to ride in the canoe when the water is calm, but see who hangs in there when it gets a little choppy and you're asked to do your share of the rowing to get you through the hard times. That's why I stay in this union – the people and the idea that we will see better times again."

John E. Curnow, member

With the union's own general fund in trouble, Business Manager Stapleton took the brave step of proposing a dues increase to combat financial losses and provide better service. His proposals were eventually voted on and passed by the membership at large.

In 1996, Stapleton retired after running Local 3 for 14 years. He was one of the most-respected business managers in Local 3 history. During his reign, he started the Geographic and Market Area Committee to allow the union and employers to adjust wages and work rules to make the union contractor competitive. He boosted retirement benefits, diversified the union's investment portfolio, started the Basic Crafts Health Care Coalition, kept Hawaii's membership with Local 3, and carried on the tradition set by Dale Marr of winning the Spirit of Life award from the City of Hope for outstanding support of their Occupational Health Department.

In August 1996, the officers voted unanimously to appoint Don Doser as business manager. Doser played a large part in getting the Rule of 85 incorporated into the union's

▲ *Business Manager Don Doser, second from left, stands with members and agents in District 80 in 1997.*

pension plan that became effective on January 1, 1997. He would continue to upgrade the plan throughout his tenure. The Rule of 85 applies to those members whose age and years of service add up to 85. If they meet the criteria, they are able to retire with a full pension. He also put in place an aggressive top-down organizing plan in 1997 that helped the union gain control of Wyoming-based Local 800.

In 1998, with the union general fund close to running out of money, language changes made to the bylaws and approved by the membership allowed Local 3 to negotiate supplemental dues into the new contracts being negotiated at the time. These supplemental dues allowed Local 3 to remain solvent as expenses rose dramatically and to hire additional staff to serve the members.

Necessity is the mother of invention, as the saying goes, and Local 3 members had some nifty inventions of their own during the '90s. The following are some examples of creative solutions to common problems born from years in the trades:

• James Western invented the Boot Pal, a handy device designed to help those with a bad back pull off their work boots or cowboy boots. He made the device by welding three separate pieces of 3/8-inch steel bar together. The invention allowed you to slip your boots on and off without having to bend over.

• The Willie Rod, a well-known invention of Willie Lee, is a surveying device that made grade setting easier, faster, and more accurate with cut and fill graduations painted red and blue.

Local 3's public employees serving as deputies at the Oakland Coliseum had their own claim to fame. During the 1990s, they became well known to the public for their diligent efforts to control the infamously rowdy crowds at the Raiders' games. Nearly 58,000 of these exuberant and often drunken fans had a habit of storming the stadium, many of them wearing skeleton face paint and covered in tattoos—pretending to be modern-day pirates.

About 54 deputy sheriffs were noted in the *Engineers News* for their security operations and particularly for dealing with the Black Hole, an informal Raider "booster club" with a not-so-spotless reputation for violence. NFL representatives were so impressed with these Local 3 members that they sent them a letter requesting they extend their security operations approach to other stadiums.

▲ *Members pose for group shot in August 1996.*

Despite all of the fun and games, the United States had become the most economically stratified industrialized nation in the world. The gap between the rich and poor surpassed Europe, including England and France—a milestone reached primarily because corporate America sent jobs overseas and used independent, non-union contractors who performed substandard work at a lower rate.

In 1979, the median weekly earnings ranged from $215 for workers with less than a secondary school education to $348 for college graduates. In 1998, that range was $337 to $821. Even as this gap widened, many employers fought increases in the federally imposed minimum wage, and Local 3 was no different. Operating Engineers have always been fighters.

Throughout the '90s, Local 3 faced adversity in many forms, from internal politics and battles with the government to dealing with the media and Mother Nature herself, but each time, this adversity was met. Local 3 ran its own media campaign to combat the claim of union corruption and started its own Web site articulating their skills and programs on the World Wide Web. When a crane collapsed in San Francisco, they spearheaded crane certification and safety classes. When prevailing wages were attacked, they marched in a throng of thousands, laying claim on the importance of a fair wage for all.

At the end of the '90s, the strength of the economy seemed to soar as unemployment fell to 4.1 percent. The abundance of jobs restored confidence that America was still a land of opportunity. Additionally, massive new housing developments allowed more people to own their own homes but they often commuted from rural areas. Local 3 benefited from this trend. Population increases always lead to a need for infrastructure improvements.

These were booming times, and toward the end of the decade, money seemed to be readily available to a growing population. It was also a decade noted for industry advancements that surpassed expectations. With all the signs pointing towards a bright 21st century, and technology advancing by leaps and bounds, Local 3 focused on the future with confidence, unaware, as was the rest of nation, of what was to come.

The 21st century began with what appeared to be a strong U.S. economy, thanks to the boom years of the late 1990s. The technological marvel known as the Internet became more mainstream, and brought with it the "dotcom" boom. The boom would soon change to bust for many companies and individuals who had been flush with cash from speculative technology enterprises. They saw their values quickly rise and then tragically plummet. Greedy corporate citizens were breaking down the norms of the working class and as a result were destined for failure.

With stunning speed, inequities between the rich and the working class, promoted by deregulation of the financial institutions and a free market agenda, brought about the single biggest financial crisis that Local 3 and the entire nation would face since the Great Depression. But, Local 3, a union born during the Great Depression, a union formed by rivals, would have the tools and the moxie to weather the storm.

In the beginning of the new century, the prosperity of the 1990s had created fabulous wealth for a small, select group of executives and wealthy shareholders, leaving an abundance of low-wage jobs for far too many Americans. The Republican free market forced lower taxes for the rich, created policies that supported outsourcing, enacted free-trade agreements, and tried to weaken unions by diminishing workers' freedom to choose a union and have a voice in politics. America was rapidly becoming a rich man's world.

During the 2000 presidential election, Local 3 heavily endorsed Democratic candidate, Vice President Al Gore. George W. Bush, like his father, ran on the same platform of lower taxes and deregulation and Local 3 had not forgotten the anti-union politics of the Republican candidate's father, George H. W. Bush. He was a rich man's son with a rich man's habits. Despite union efforts, following a heavily contested election, Bush

Opposite Page ◄ San Francisco Bay Bridge construction in 2007. ▲ Climbing the rails on the Golden Gate Bridge in November 2008.

moved into the White House in January 2001. What would follow—September 11, the Iraq War, Hurricane Katrina, the collapse of the financial markets—would decimate the economy. It would take the election of Barack Obama in 2008 to finally bring hope to the union.

In 2001, as the political climate began to darken, Local 3 spearheaded a new political program, the Operating Engineers Community Action Team (OE CAT), a name coined in August 2001 by Ron Bucholz. Thanks in part to OE CAT, Sacramento scored a $360 million Project Labor Agreement (PLA) project with Sacramento Municipal Utilities District (SMUD) to build a 500-megawatt power plant at Rancho Seco.

The Rancho Seco project, plus work from a four-year, $5 billion transportation funding package proposed by California Governor Gray Davis, meant an abundance of future jobs for Local 3. Included in the transportation project would be a fourth bore to the Caldecott Tunnel on Highway 24 between Alameda and Contra Costa counties and a BART extension from Fremont to downtown San Jose. However, these projects would not even break ground

Above Left ▲ *A crane lifts a windmill into place in April 2003. Above Right* ▲ *Quarry work in District 70 in October 2005. Opposite Page* ▶ *Nighttime paving is common to decrease traffic congestion during construction.*

"*Members always drive the union. Retirees will vote. They see through the crap. They aren't fooled.*"

Rob Wise, former officer

until later in the decade. It was the need for massive housing developments, brought about by a housing shortage and the subsequent rise in prices, which would bring immediate jobs for Local 3.

Due in part to this unprecedented real estate boom, Local 3 reached its highest membership number since inception with more than 37,000 members. One of the largest jobs these members worked on was the reshaping of 6,000 acres of Dougherty Valley in Contra Costa County, a project that was projected to last 33 years and pave the way for 11,700 houses. As a sign of the times, the "Swap Shop" stopped listing houses for sale. Real estate was being gobbled up like candy—often selling for more than the asking price—and needed no advertisement.

Above ▲ *A work crew stands inside a concrete pipe at the Hetch Hetchy Dam in October 2003.* *Right* ▶ *An aerial view of a crane from the Hetch Hetchy Dam.*

When the 2000 year-end figures were calculated, California's construction industry had its fourth consecutive double-digit increase, $61.64 billion, up 12 percent from 1999, including both private and public works.

Throughout its history, Local 3 had overcome many challenges—natural and man-made disasters, foreign wars, political assaults, internal strife, environmentalists, and economic downturns. But nothing could prepare Local 3 or any American for what happened on September 11, 2001. Still reeling in disbelief, as day after day, footage of the carnage played again and again on every television channel, Local 3 announced a blood drive for victims. They also urged members to remember and honor their fellow brothers and sisters, members of the IUOE, working in New York and Washington DC. Many IUOE members, including Local 3 member B. K. Cooper, actually worked on the cleanup at Ground Zero following the attacks. Their selfless actions on this often dangerous and sad operation prompted Chaplain Ray Giunta to call the Operating Engineers "the heroes of Ground Zero."

In response to the attacks, Congress passed the Homeland Security Act in November 2002—an act to strengthen America's borders and keep the country safe, but at a cost to union workers. Workers could be fired at will, denied government jobs, and prohibited from organizing. The act was passed despite union opposition. However, Local 3 again stepped up to the plate in defense of their country. Recognizing that another 9/11-style attack was possible, they joined forces with California Fire and Rescue personnel in joint disaster-response training held in McClellan, California. Local 3's relationship with fire and rescue professionals would eventually lead to disaster-response training at the RMTC.

As 2001 came to an end, final preparations were under way for the 2002 Winter Olympic Games in Utah, a project started in the '90s. The Olympics gave a still grieving nation a brief respite. It would also give a boost to Utah's economy. From downtown Salt Lake City, where thousands of Olympic fans and athletes slept, to the snow-covered nearby Wasatch Mountains, Utah's residents reaped a bonanza of capital improvements thanks to Local 3.

Also that year, Local 3 participated in the needed renovation of state capitol buildings in Sacramento, including the completion of the Capitol Area East End Complex, the largest single government complex in California history with a 1.5 million-square-foot office complex and a lush 40-acre park. There was also plenty of bridge work to go around for Local 3. In Crockett, California, work on the old Carquinez Bridge, built in 1927, had begun. The 3,465-foot suspension bridge needed to be replaced in order to carry traffic westbound on I-80. Since breaking ground, the project averaged 120 workers per day, 30 of which were Operating Engineers. By September 4, 2007, all of the original 1927 steel structures had been demolished—a feat that paid good wages but left the surrounding Crockett-area residents saddened by the disappearance of a bridge steeped in history.

The Benicia Bridge, the link between Benicia, California, to the north with Martinez to the south, opened in 1962. In 2007, a 1.7-mile bridge was built alongside to carry five lanes of northbound traffic at a cost of $1.3 billion. The bridge is part of I-680, a major transportation link. One of the most awe-inspiring bridge projects was the Bay Bridge expansion, which broke ground in January 2002. The $2.6 billion project kept more than 120 operators busy on what was deemed "the largest ongoing bridge project in the Western Hemisphere." The skyway part of the bridge alone was worth more than $1 billion, the largest construction contract ever awarded by Caltrans. Ongoing work on the bridge continues today.

Above ▲ *San Francisco Bay Bridge construction in December 2004. Opposite Page* ▶ *Cranes tower above the new bridge construction on the Benicia Bridge in November 2004.*

The boom in membership meant an increased need for training centers. And so, new training centers began to spring up all over the local's jurisdiction, including Wyoming and South Dakota. Local 3 had plans to put into place apprenticeship programs for these two states, which at first showed some promise. Several Native American reservations, including the Lower Brule tribe in South Dakota, showed interest in working with Local 3 to train their own in exchange for land. But once the program began, it was apparent there was no work for these apprentices. The training site was moved from South Dakota to Casper, Wyoming, where less environmental regulations meant more and quicker projects. Those graduating from the center were the most sought-after in the state because of their skills. However, eventually there were fiscal problems and Wyoming and South Dakota's inclusion in Local 3's jurisdiction ended.

Construction on Hawaii's 108-acre training center in Kahuku began in 2002 at an estimated cost of $6.25 million. Since 1994, training had occurred on some 15 acres adjacent to the site. Training sites appeared in Nevada as well. In 2001, Local 3 bought a 153-acre site in Wadsworth as home for the center. Water rights on the site made it a goldmine, since the 212 acre-feet of water from an underground aquifer had a potential value of $1 million. In June 2003, the center opened.

With all the work coming in from the housing industry, infrastructure improvements and the public works sector, organizing was essential and ongoing. For example, in November 2002, the biggest organizing victory in Local 3's history occurred when a joint-trench construction company of about 400 hourly employees signed an agreement after a three-year campaign.

Unlike the 1990s, which was markedly all-quiet on the strike front, so far the first decade of the 21st century has provided plenty of picket-line drama. Unfortunately, although unions have been gaining ground politically and gaining clout, not all labor disputes have congenial outcomes. For example, members working at a mine in northeastern

Nevada had worked without a contract for more than a year. In response to their request, the employer pushed an unfair contract, provoking an embarrassing two-day strike near corporate headquarters.

In Reno, Nevada, it would take a baby's kidnapping to bring dangerous working conditions at the Washoe Medical Center to light. The kidnapping resulted in a trial, at which Local 3 members and nurses of the HealthCare Division testified against the hospital, stating that conditions and the nurse-to-patient ratio were to blame for the child's kidnapping.

In the summer of 2001, Reno nurses staged a historic strike to improve patient care. The strike was featured on every Reno TV station and newspaper. The nurses had joined the union in 1999 in an effort to improve conditions, but negotiations with the hospital fell apart shortly thereafter. Finally, the nurses staged a one-day strike in June 2001, as Washoe Medical hired scab nurses to fill their slots. Eventually, after striking again in August, the nurses were awarded $1 million in back pay with a court decision that allowed "union representatives to participate in employee grievance hearings, halt questioning employees about union activities and cease the unlawful prohibition on union solicitation in its cafeteria." Local 3 no longer represents nurses.

▲ *Nevada nurses strike in 2001.*

As in previous decades, in 2003 there would be problems at the 12th largest copper producer in the world. After 250 people gathered at the Utah state capitol to support Kennecott employees and health and welfare benefits for Kennecott retirees, the company was forced back to the bargaining table to continue contract negotiations. Eventually, these workers approved a six-year contract that guaranteed Kennecott would not contract out, or outsource, its employees. Another ongoing battle was with a Texas mining company. This non-union company tried for decades to dominate northern California's rock, sand, and gravel industry by attempting to control the road leading to the largest single construction-grade aggregate in the western United States. More than 2.3 billion tons of sand and gravel worth at least $15 billion lay in the Yuba Goldfields, a nine-mile stretch of the Yuba River east of Marysville. Western Aggregates tried to stake exclusive claim to this resource.

After a hard-fought battle, a Yuba County Superior Court judge denied the company's claim to the road, meaning union employers could now compete for the rights to mine sand and gravel in the goldfields. The battle continued through 2004 when the Operating Engineers JAC started negotiations with the Bureau of Land Management (BLM) to lease the fields for training specialized in the rock, sand, and gravel industry. This was a big victory for Local 3 because new rock, sand, and gravel plants continue to spring up all over its jurisdiction in order to provide supplies for the unending improvement of roads and subdivisions.

The Superior Court also declared Hammonton Road through Yuba Goldfield a public road, clearing the way for a possible training center for Local 3. This center would be planned in conjunction with the residents of Yuba and Sutter counties. In January 2006, the Marysville City Council endorsed the application of 57 acres in the Yuba Goldfields for the construction of a year-round heavy equipment operator training center.

In 2005, while thousands of Louisiana National Guard troops searched for terrorists in Iraq and Afghanistan, a major disaster hit their home state and its neighbor, Mississippi. One of the five deadliest hurricanes ever to hit the mainland, Katrina, formed over the Bahamas on August 23, crossing southern Florida before strengthening rapidly in the Gulf of Mexico. On August 29, it struck southeast Louisiana, causing the levees protecting New Orleans to fail. At least 1,836 people lost their lives. Thousands of others were left homeless, jobless, and in despair.

Local 3 contributed to Hurricane Katrina victims through the IUOE Hurricane Katrina Relief Fund, collecting more than $223,000 for victims, some of whom were Operating Engineers. Like Retiree Rob Roy, whose poignant testimony says it all: "We're at least alive, lost everything but found in the mud and debris my equipment keys that retired with me and my Local 3 belt buckle. It's amazing what salt water can do; it turns everything to rust and corrosion in a matter of hours, but it's just stuff, and we will survive."

In California state politics, a hurricane of popular opinion had turned against democratic governor Davis, fueled by the tremendous charisma and deep pockets of Hollywood action figure Arnold Schwarzenegger. The campaign to recall Davis started in July 2003, and although Local 3 stood behind Davis in the October 7, 2003 recall election, the "Terminator" had no trouble bumping him from his seat.

Like Ronald Reagan, his fellow actor, at first Schwarzenegger attempted to woo the unions. To applause from union members at a huge press conference in Pittsburg, California, the new governor promised that he would fully fund Proposition 42, a gas-tax measure earmarked for transportation funding that had been in jeopardy. But Schwarzenegger didn't stay in the union's good graces for long. In 2005, his so-called special election was plagued with initiatives intended to silence working people. Thanks in part to Local 3's political action, all initiatives were thwarted. Schwarzenegger's popularity with the union would continue to decline, as California state budget problems worsened.

In union politics, Don Doser won the election in August 2003, and in November of the same year, announced he was stepping down as business manager for medical reasons. John Bonilla, then president, was appointed to complete Doser's unfinished term as business manager. Bonilla's term as business manager came at a difficult time in state politics with the recently elected governor causing a shift in the mood in Sacramento. Bonilla was not new to the politics at the

Opposite Page ◀ A large concrete pour in October 2007. Top Right ▶ Arnold Schwarzenegger walking with members of Local 3. Bottom Right ▶ Business Manager John Bonilla at a press conference for Proposition 42 in 2005.

state level and made some attempts at compromises with the new administration, appearing at a number of high-profile jobsites and press conferences, but this did not last long as the state budget worsened.

The difficult economic climate and plummeting stock market eventually led to the need for modifications to the Local 3 Pension Plan. The pension trustees were forced to reduce the benefit accrual rate to 1.15 percent, 1.75 percent, or 3 percent, to be voted on by the individual bargaining units. As can be expected, when the DVD presentation, "Straight Talk About Your Pension" was shown at district meetings to explain the situation, it was met with many questions and concerns regarding the union's retirement reserves.

Bonilla had some support early in his term as business manager and was looking forward to his next term. But when his own set of officers were unable to support him, and an investigation turned up damaging evidence of fiscal mismanagement in a report that became known as the "Faris Report," the handwriting was on the wall for his hopes of being elected by an increasingly irate membership. Details about the Doser payout when he stepped down as business manager cast doubt on the financial practices of Bonilla and Doser and would eventually lead to legal actions against them both.

In response to legal findings and ongoing conflicts in the Bonilla administration, the split in the support of the officers resulted in an unprecedented landslide victory for the ticket known as the "Gold Ticket." The entire slate of officers and the related positions on their ticket were elected in what was an overwhelming mandate for change. Business Manager Russ Burns, President Fred Herschbach,

▲ *Swearing in ceremony of the "Gold Ticket" on September 1, 2006.*

Vice President Carl Goff, Recording Corresponding Secretary Rob Wise, Financial Secretary Jim Sullivan, and Treasurer Dan Reding won in a landslide victory after campaigning on a ticket of transparency and fiscal responsibility. The membership voted in large numbers in what was a historic election for Local 3.

Immediately after being sworn into office, the new administration began the hard work of winning back the trust of the membership. In November 2006, the *Engineers News* published an update on a lawsuit filed against Doser. Malpractice charges were filed against Doser's attorneys who counterclaimed that Bonilla had collaborated with Doser. It was a mess. Eventually, Doser was ordered to pay damages and forfeit future pension benefits. The court ruled that he improperly took union funds for his own personal gain.

▼ *Surveyors working on a housing development in May 2007.*

Burns later recalled the election as "very heated and divisive." Some members contested the election results, but a later Department of Labor investigation proved that the results were accurate. Burns' Gold Ticket platform was comprised of certain concepts, including a member-elected bylaws committee, a system of checks and balances, a staff compensation review, published quarterly financial reports, and details on the State of the Union.

During the first 2½ years of tenure, the Gold Ticket systematically crossed these platform items off the list and added even more along the way. For instance, in order to improve communications with the membership, they added a "Letters to the Editor" section in *Engineers News*. Additionally, in regular and special-called district meetings of members during their first year of tenure, they recommended changes to the dues portion (Article VI) of the bylaws, thus giving $5.3 million back to the membership in dues reductions. Additional changes to the bylaws were approved by the membership to ensure ongoing transparency to the membership.

▼ *Stockton members work on the Union Ranch project.*

Local 3's political OE CAT was changed to Voice of the Engineer (VOTE) in 2007 to clarify the change in the new administration's agenda and leadership role. Same concept, different title, better prizes: to build power and strength for working people through the election of labor-friendly candidates and legislation. Retiree Ken Green was noted for coming up with the name decades ago.

One of the longest-running strikes in Local 3's history was against Valley Power Systems North, Inc., a heavy-duty repair facility in San Leandro, California. The company had taken over the shop in September 2005 and failed to honor the union wage and benefit package that had been in place for many years. The strike began in July 2007, nearly two years after the company took over with numerous attempts to reach an agreement. These workers

Above ▲ *Moving the earth during the widening of Highway 149 in Butte County, California.* *Top Right* ▶ *A work crew responsible for widening Highway 149 in Butte County in May 2006.* *Bottom Right* ▶ *After years of delays, work finally began on widening Highway 149 in Butte County in May 2006.*

had chosen to be represented by a union for some 45 years, but, despite an existing contract, were thwarted at every turn. They had no choice but to strike, a strike that continued for more than 90 weeks and was taken to the doorsteps of their facilities in Fresno, West Sacramento, and the company's headquarters in City of Industry.

The strike brought together many unions—including representatives from Local 12 and Local 612 known as the "West Coast Wall" of Operating Engineers—labor activists, community supporters, and public officials. The union began a weekly publication, *The Picket Line Press*, which was featured every quarter in the IUOE magazine, *The International*. Supporters contributed more than $125,000 to the strike fund.

On April 1, 2009, as the facility in San Leandro closed its doors for good, the union held its last rally out front, commending the strikers and supporters for helping rid the area of another unwanted "rat." To date, this was the union's longest strike, spearheading a strike fund and improving relationships with the media and the public that will far outlast the ill effects of Valley Power's union-busting ways.

▶ *Members drill 2,200 rock columns with a stone-column machine in Crescent City.*

A worldwide recession that continues into Local 3's 70th year has made jobs scarce and money short at every level, while health-care costs continue to rise nationwide. In response, Local 3 has begun work on preventive health-care measures with a health intelligence and solutions company. Working together, they created a program to empower members to be responsible for their own health and to make lifestyle changes designed to increase longevity and improve their quality of life, while cutting down on health-care costs. The wellness concept has taken on a larger sponsor with the IUOE getting involved in the hopes of educating the entire international membership in the benefits of wellness and disease management.

Other buzzwords or acronyms in our increasingly busy world that came into play during the new decade included the Pension Protection Act (PPA). This act, signed into law by Bush in 2006, was meant to be the rulebook for pension plans. It dictates what trustees can and cannot do regarding pensions and provides different indicators of when a plan is in trouble and in jeopardy of being taken over by the Pension Benefit Guaranty Corporation (PBGC), a federal corporation established by the Employee Retirement Income Security Act of 1974.

◀ *Drill Operator Jim Dallara and Oiler Ron Cross drill a pier for a new bridge as part of the Highway 1/Confusion Hill realignment.*

The complicated act contains standards for judging the viability of a pension's plans; plans fall either in a green, yellow, or red zone based on how they match each standard.

In April 2008, members learned that their pension fund fell in the "yellow" zone, or close to 80 percent funded. Changes to the current plan had to be made in order to avoid falling into the red zone. These changes, which were announced in a series of springtime meetings, were effective July 1, 2008, with the same benefit factor for all participants, now 1.25 percent of all contributions.

With the economy worsening, work hours deteriorating in one of the most severe declines in the history of Local 3, and lenders tightening their reigns on what was once considered "hocus pocus" lending laws, the unions turned in force to support the Democratic nominee for president, Barack Obama. For members in California, where the state budget was already more than five months late and over budget to

▲ *Barack Obama in Hawaii wearing a Local 3 hat in August 2008.* Background Photo ▼ *Dredging the Alameda channel in the San Francisco Bay in February 2008.*

the tune of billions of dollars, the situation was especially dire. It's no wonder that Local 3 turned to the November 2008 election like a weary traveler turns to the light. That light did shine.

After hundreds of volunteer hours in Local 3's four-state jurisdiction, the change the union rallied for—political strength, infrastructure funding, and tax relief for the middle class—became a reality. In November 2008, Obama was elected the 44th president of the United States. Local 3's political efforts helped turned the once-red state of Nevada blue thanks to weekends spent walking neighborhoods and spreading the word about the nation's new hope for change. The Democratic president had labor at the top of his list.

The 2008 General Election brought the entire union together to campaign for the change the country and the labor movement desperately needed, and they were successful. They came together in new ways of political activism, looking toward the future with new hope.

During the first decade of the 21st century, the union has faced both external and internal turmoil. The eight-year term of George W. Bush, coupled with national disasters, two wars, a housing bust, and California's budget crisis, created a dark climate,

Retiree picnic at Rancho Murieta Training Center in June 2008. ▼ *Strike at Granite Rock in 2004.*

"One of the most important things for the future of this local is ensuring that we continue to have the most qualified, trained staff in the labor industry. And that we train the best operating engineers in terms of skills and knowledge that are available to the employers."

Russ Burns, business manager

while internal union politics clouded many members' images of what their union was all about. But Local 3 weathered the storms and emerged stronger, steadier, and more streamlined. Today, Local 3 continues to evolve, adjusting to the shifting political, technological, and social climate of this nation while breaking new ground.

Above Top ▲ *Hawaii road work in August 2008. Above Bottom* ▲ *Business Manager Russ Burns speaks at the final Valley Power Rally on April 1, 2009.*

171

PROLOGUE  *by Mandy Jo Jessup*

A historical account is just that, an account, a story. Many of the details outlined in this book came first as stories—so much of the labor movement is fixed in oral history. While the book is filled with details and dates from labor's history, it is also an account of national history, which ever-affected the successes and struggles of this union and its members.

We ask that you pause for a moment in thinking on this history—the political ramifications of the cold war or the hardship of internal union politics—and remember what this history is really about: a snapshot perhaps of a sunburned, sweat-stained face in the seat of a rig, grading acres of earth, shaping the backdrop for what would remain long after that person passes on. The history of Operating Engineers rests not only in the stories told on early-morning jobsites over strong coffee but also in the very landscape of bridges and bypasses we use every day.

This book also proves that because of natural disasters, even those built landmarks are not always permanent. They can be blown away by hurricanes or turned to ash from fires. But what is permanent are the stories told through letters, old photos, and newspaper articles. That's why a book of this nature is so important, and why the stories these members shared are priceless.

This history is also about an organization born of necessity. Unions did not come about from boredom or the need for fraternal organizations. They came about because people were living—and dying—in terrible working conditions without any protection or representation. Today, an Operating Engineer makes a respectable wage with good benefits, and he retires with dignity—ask any one of the retirees who contributed to this book and they will agree. They will also agree that this is their finest legacy.

During Local 3's 70 years, working-class Americans paved the way, struggled, grew, changed, forged ahead, and weathered politics, wars, Mother Nature, and their own internal differences to emerge stronger than when they began with decades of history to prove it.

This book is just the beginning. They've only just broke ground.

Opposite Page ▶ *In Fresno, members pose on the front of a Bucyrus 636 dragline. They include, from left: Chad Montgomery, Lyn Parker, Mike Donaldson, Do Ngo, Juan Lazaro, Mike Corazzini, Bill Williams, Romero Perez, Gilber Quintana, Robert Wiebe, Garret Azares, Oscar Steelman, and Jack Schildberg.*

"*The road ahead will be long. Our climb will be steep. We may not get there in one year or even one term, but America...we will get there. ...I will ask you to join in the work of remaking this nation the only way it's been done in America for 221 years – block by block, brick by brick, calloused hand by calloused hand.*"

Barack Obama

173

"It is important to pause and take a look at where we came from, and where we are going. History allows us to look in the mirror, to take our pulse and, in doing so, shed light on our present and investigate our vision of where we can go in the future as an organization. It allows us to laugh, to remember the good times and the bad, to tell stories, and to take a look at the many challenges that have been a part of the history of this incredible union."

Russ Burns, business manager

INDEX

▲ *TS 14 scraper working on the California Aqueduct. (Courtesy of Sandy Steele, daughter of Gerald "Jerry" Steele)*